MEMPHIS
200 YEARS TOGETHER

MEMPHIS

200 YEARS TOGETHER

EDITED BY

KAREN B. GOLIGHTLY

& JONATHAN JUDAKEN

FOREWORD BY LEE HARRIS

SUSAN SCHADT PRESS

MEMPHIS | NEW ORLEANS

Published in 2019 by

Susan Schadt Press, LLC

© 2019 Karen B. Golightly and Jonathan Judaken

We acknowledge with deep gratitude Maysey Craddock's gracious contribution of the cover art for this anthology.

Cover art "a thousand rivers I" © 2011 Maysey Craddock.

Graphic Design: Reid Mitchell, Memphis

Library of Congress Control Number 2019938256

ISBN 978-1-7336341-0-6

Printed by Friesens, Altona, Canada

TABLE OF CONTENTS

FOREWORD:
REFLECTIONS ON THE MEMPHIS BICENTENNIAL

Memphis deserves a birthday.

Birthdays are celebrations of history, progress, challenge, growth.

As the chapters in this volume suggest, our community has had all that and more.

Memphis is a remarkable American city. It's the large southern metropolis on the Mississippi River that is physically at the edge of Tennessee's southwestern tip but has always felt to me like a place at the center of the universe.

Birthdays are a chance to toot your horn a bit, crow over accomplishments, listen as people sing your praises.

If you're lucky, people literally sing to you.

Our city deserves all of that and more.

Birthdays are also excuses for reinvention.

Memphis has reinvented itself time and time again through the years. It has faced down tremendous existential threats — yellow fever, the Memphis Massacre, lynching, the King assassination — that would have devastated any other place. Yet, each time the city finds a way to turn the corner and order up a makeover.

Even in architecture and planning and development, Memphians have become adept at repurpose, reuse, and reinvention.

Downtown Memphis today, for instance, has been reimagined and revitalized as forgotten and arguably useless structures get a chance at a second act.

Memphis is probably the only place in America where an old postal building is now our University's law school.

For years, our downtown skyline included a long-mothballed downtown basketball stadium shaped like a pyramid and nicknamed the Tomb of Doom. The Tomb of Doom has been reborn and today it's a mega-retail store for fishing and hunting enthusiasts. I'm not making that up.

Although markers of the past, birthdays are special because they are filled with promise and say something about the future.

Birthdays are filled with impossible contradictions and raise uncomfortable questions. They are reason to celebrate and feast on cake.

They are also, frankly, sometimes reason to mourn the loss of time and pledge to diet.

For most adults, birthdays give reason to consider how much time is actually left to accomplish what one wants in terms of career or travel. How much time is left to take pictures of the kids, to hug someone, or to find someone or something to love?

For our city, this 200th birthday will inevitably force us to consider how much progress has been made on our main issues: crime, poverty, and race.

As an elected official, I'm not afraid to concede that it will likely be the grassroots (non-elected) activists who raise those uncomfortable questions as we celebrate this birthday, and it wouldn't be the first time.

It was city sanitation workers in the 1960s that led a strike that brought Martin Luther King Jr. to Memphis in 1968, where he was assassinated, an event that marked one of the most important turning points in the civil rights movement.

I could draw a straight-line from that history to today's push among activists for a living wage of fifteen dollars per hour, the removal of Confederate monuments from city parks, or the most recent movement in our city, known as MICAH, where people of faith are coming together to make government focus on our most urgent problems.

This birthday is important, because it marks a new chapter in public dialogue.

I've lived in Memphis for almost my entire life, and my roots run deep. We are in a moment that feels like the first time most Memphians are all on the same page.

We are in a period where Memphians, both young and young at heart, wealthy and hopeful, Black and White, families who have been here for generations and millennials who have just moved here, all seem to realize that we are in this thing together.

We are together.

We are in a period where whether you live in the sprawling suburbs or the urban core, you know we have to focus on poverty and inequality.

In fact, we're in a period where virtually everyone agrees on the really important public policy topics. We should invest more in early childhood education so kids don't start behind. We have to fix public transit so people can get to work and get home at a reasonable hour for dinner with the family. We have to expand fairness in our criminal justice system.

We are in a period of agreement that a new generation of leaders, preachers, politicians, athletes, entertainers, entrepreneurs, writers, and activists have really emerged.

It's a New Era.

We know our history but we are prepared to forge a new path. We are tired of the tired politics of yesterday.

Our best and brightest are increasingly returning home to Memphis after many decades of living and thriving elsewhere. They are ready for opportunity right now, right here in Memphis. And they aren't afraid to break the china.

Most importantly, we have broad agreement that our community should embrace its diversity and confront division.

We haven't always been so poised for agreement and progress.

We haven't always had so much reason for hope.

In fact, it wasn't too long ago that division and segregation permeated our local government, with a relatively White "county government" and a Black "city government." In today's Memphis, however, we have a Black county mayor and White city mayor.

It may surprise those who think they know our town to read that in today's Memphis tropes about our city are constantly being dismantled and turned upside down.

But the best birthdays come with surprises.

LEE HARRIS
MAYOR OF SHELBY COUNTY

To Jaynie, Julia, Joelle, Bella, Phin, and Pip, and all of the other Memphians who make this place home. And to colleagues and collegiality, to those represented in these pages and to the community of writers and scholars who elevate the world by being teachers and lifelong learners.

CHAPTER ONE

INTRODUCTION:
A COUNTER-MONUMENT TO MEMPHIS

Karen B. Golightly and Jonathan Judaken

Near downtown Memphis on December 20, 2017, in the middle of the night, crews removed monuments to three Confederate leaders. Like thousands of such statues erected throughout the South at the height of segregation, these stone fossils were intended to petrify the values of White supremacy that arose in the aftermath of the Civil War, reinforcing the racial legacy upon which our nation was founded.* The resistance to these ever-present reminders of racial inequality and injustice has ebbed and flowed like the waters of the Mississippi that shape the landscape of our city.

Like many other southern towns, Memphis has been obsessed with these monuments in recent years — some declaring them representations of our city's past, others claiming them a disgrace to our city's present. Each memorial served as a haunting reminder of where we've been as a city and as a people. But as Memphis approached the fiftieth anniversary of the 1968 assassination of Dr. Martin Luther King Jr., city officials, responding to public pressure, ultimately agreed that such prominent symbols of segregation were not only a civic embarrassment but a visible repudiation of the beloved community of equality that Dr. King preached. The statues of Nathan Bedford Forrest, J. Harvey Mathes, and Jefferson Davis were removed, leaving empty plinths in their place — mini-stages upon which Memphis could play out a different future. This book could be fittingly placed onto that empty space.

Like statues and memorials, this book straddles the relationship between the past and the present, memory and power. But a book is not built in stone and cement. Statues "are how people are placed in hierarchies, how social stratification is made to seem inevitable and right, how feelings of inferiority and superiority are engendered, and how indifference to

---

* Throughout this book, we have capitalized both Black and White in the same way that Asian, Hispanic, Arab, and Jewish identify socially constructed or socially recognized groupings, since these designations function analogously within Memphis culture. In the chapters that were previously published or in quotations from prior works that did not capitalize Black or White, we have not altered the spelling of those prior publications.

violence against those on the bottom is rationalized and normalized. Social supremacy is made, inside and between people, through making meanings."[1] A book makes meaning otherwise.

This book, then, is better understood as a counter-monument. It offers not a set script, but a series of stories about where we have been, what it has meant, and how it has shaped the culture of Memphis. It is a confluence of multiple voices with diverse perspectives commemorating 200 years together in Memphis, even when so much of that history was shaped by forced separation. Rather than built in stone, this counter-monument is more like the Mississippi River that winds through our topography, whispering to us rather than berating us, it is more like a throughway than a set piece.

Like the Mississippi River that holds tight to our banks, these stories, written by many pens with different viewpoints, engage the currents that have shaped our past, present, and future. History, photography, music, food, sports, business, religion, and education have influenced our lived experience in Memphis. All these facets of our lives have privileged some and marginalized others, but often in ways unexpected and ever-shifting. This flow cannot be encapsulated in monuments built in stone. The malleability of the page shows the meandering history of Memphis and its people.

The emblem of our counter-monument is embossed on the cover. The title of Maysie Craddock's artwork, "a thousand rivers I," summarizes the key theme of the stories recounted in this book. Craddock, a visual artist and native Memphian, draws upon the rivers and landscape of this region in order to transport "the viewer into a meditative place that is nostalgic and rhythmic, yet fragile, hopeful, and wild — an opportunity to begin, again."[2]

If it is to aid us in moving forward, a counter-memorial should have a paradoxical relationship to the past. Our trip down memory lane must be shaped by our desire for the memories we want to have in the future. Craddock's abstractions, built upon the winding landscape of real rivers, conjure such a future-oriented memorializing. They can take us on journeys in many directions. This is the power not only of art, but of books.

This volume was conceived and produced by Memphis Reads, whose motto is "creating community one book at a time." Since its founding in 2014, Memphis Reads has chosen one author and one book for a citywide read, bringing together universities, businesses, organizations, schools, museums, the city government, and most important, readers. Each book gives us a way to explore new worlds and universal issues that make us all human. This year, to celebrate the bicentennial of the founding of Memphis, we wanted to showcase the many byways that run through our city. No one book or single author contained the multitude of stories that define the major tributaries of our culture. So we decided to create such a book.

Memphis: 200 Years Together was built by people from Memphis for people from Memphis. It was also created to showcase the breadth and depth of Memphis to those travelers — real and virtual — who find their way to our shores on the Mississippi. Not only the artist, but the publisher, the distributor, the contributors, the editors, and the designer all come from Memphis or are long-time residents of the city or the state. This is a gathering of some of the leading scholars, writers, and cultural creators in the region.

Memphis: 200 Years Together highlights the ebb and flow of Memphis' past and how it has seeped into the city's present identity. It begins with the first peoples of Memphis, the Chickasaw. The book moves from the city's founding to the centrality of cotton to the city's economy and to the history of slavery that came with it. It traces the course of the Civil War and the long-enduring memories and myths shaping public consciousness that underpin the battles about monuments in Memphis. It explores the tragic drama of the yellow fever epidemic and how it changed the demography of the city. Readers are invited to enter the blues joints, rock 'n' roll clubs, and soul studios that shaped the Memphis sound. They can sample not only the taste of barbecue, but how the rich array of restaurants was transformed by the migrants who wandered into town and set up shop. The spiritual sustenance they found was sheltered in the houses of worship that have impacted every aspect of life in Memphis. Religion was as much the idiom of disenfranchisement and disempowerment as it was of struggle and contestation. This found its way into politics and law, which was challenged in art as well as in music. All were key in the long freedom struggle of Blacks in Memphis, most famously in the period of the civil rights movement, and in the changing lives of Whites in the city as well. Today these struggles take place in public institutions, like schools, museums, and even parks.

Just as the past and our own lives together are entangled, so the stories themselves are intertwined with each other. G. Wayne Dowdy's overview of the development of industry and business in Memphis cannot but recount the influence of music here, which is also discussed in far more detail in

Charles L. Hughes's chapter. Jennifer Biggs's history of Memphis laying claim to the origins of barbecue is a story, in part, about the Chickasaw, and the pigs who were brought here by Spanish explorers, as well as about Black food cultures. Thus it is part of the history that runs through Beverly G. Bond and Janann Sherman's chapter on the founding of Memphis. Molly Caldwell Crosby's narrative about yellow fever describes the heroic role of ministers and nuns during the epidemic, while David Waters chronicles how religious leaders have guided the course of Memphis' culture since then. Aram Goudsouzian's tracing of the civil rights struggle in Memphis surfaces anew in Daniel Kiel's documentation about the segregation of education and Geoff Calkins' piece on the racial dynamics of basketball in our city.

Preston Lauterbach's chapter, "Memphis Burning," details the racial injustice in the history of housing in Memphis, while Zandria F. Robinson questions the stagnant representations of the past in our "chocolate city" today. If Shelby Foote and Timothy S. Huebner's chapters on the Civil War, alongside Stephen V. Ash's account of the Memphis massacre of 1866, remind us of the history of Black degradation, then Earnestine Jenkins spotlights how Black photographers sought to reshape the representation of African Americans as dignified achievers whose successes, like those of their White counterparts, were human, all too human. The stories here reflect the fight, pain, and suffering as well as the hope, persistence, and triumph of Memphians in the face of adversity. Ultimately, the contemporary motto of Memphis — "grit and grind" — runs through the larger set of narratives that we have compiled in this book.

This not a coffee table book, nor a nostalgic journey that overlooks the challenges that have defined and continue to trouble Memphis. It is a book about struggles and achievements, and the interlaced communities that have inhabited this city over the past 200 years. This is a chance to see Memphis as a whole new place, without forgetting our muddy past. Every aspect of this book is a reflection of Memphis today and a counter-monument to our past, which is as diverse as the people who live here, and runs as deep and long as the mighty Mississippi.

CHAPTER TWO

FOUNDING MEMPHIS

Beverly G. Bond and Janann Sherman

Memphis is a city in black and white, a vibrant city with a divided heart. It is a city of contrasts and contradictions where southern charm and elegance meet southern tension and violence. For much of its history, Memphis has been inhabited by and divided by two peoples who share a common place and history but are separated by the social and political differences ascribed to race.

Memphis is the capital city of the Mississippi Delta; a land of rich soil and grinding poverty. Defined and dominated by the ceaseless and unpredictable Mississippi River, the city's strategic location made it a natural distribution port and center of commerce. Settlers to the rich agricultural hinterlands around the city brought cotton culture and slave labor to the mid-South. As the gateway to the lower South and the trans-Mississippi West, Memphis became the largest inland cotton market in the world. Later development of roads, railroads, and air service sustained the city's dominance in transportation and distribution, a position reinforced in the late twentieth century by Federal Express. Memphis International Airport handles more air cargo than any other field in the world.

Memphis is a city that is progressive and provincial at the same time, a volatile mix of rich and poor, black and white, rural and urban, old and new. African Americans, once freed of legal bondage, came to the city seeking a better life. Ironically, their greatest cultural legacy—Memphis music—is a product of the misery they fled and the poverty and divisiveness they found.

As the twenty-first century begins, there are hopeful signs of the old bifurcated system breaking down. This is the result of Herculean efforts of blacks and whites to bridge the racial divide as well as the influx of other groups who have complicated the simple binary of black and white. The newest migrants to Memphis include an estimated half-million Latinos, Asians, Africans, and people from the Middle East. Cultural awareness festivals dot the social calendar; the largest of them all is the month-long Memphis in May celebration. The month begins and ends with a celebration of music: the three-day Beale Street Music Festival showcases Memphis' reputation as the Home of the Blues and the Birthplace of Rock 'n' Roll. It ends with the Sunset Symphony and Memphis family picnic on the banks of the Mississippi River. In between, we celebrate Memphis' most famous export, barbecue, with the World Championship Barbecue Contest.

Memphis remains endlessly fascinating and complex, a city that still draws people with its music, its vitality, its promise.

*****

From a strategic location high above the Mississippi River at the Fourth Bluff between Cairo, Illinois, and New Orleans, Louisiana, Memphis has been a center for transit, trade, and commerce for most of its history. Indian and European nations recognized the importance of the site and contested for power in the region long before American settlers arrived. Native Americans inhabited the region about 10,000 years ago. Over the next 9,000 years, Native-American groups moved gradually through the Archaic and Woodland stages, and in the Mississippian stage (800 A.D.) cities and primitive city-states emerged.

The most famous of these cities and city-states was Cahokia, across from the present-day site of St. Louis. Yet remains of Mississippian culture in western Tennessee have been found at Pinson Mound, 80 miles east of present-day Memphis, and at Chisca's Mound and Chucalissa in Shelby County. These sites were part of a string of towns along the Mississippi River south of present-day Memphis. Mississippian culture was characterized by trade and a growing reliance on corn cultivation, sizable concentrations of populations, social stratification, hereditary chiefdoms, and the construction of large flat-top mounds. These mounds were used as platforms for temples and as the living quarters for chiefs and priests.

The town of Chucalissa (Choo-kah-le-sah) was established around 1000 A.D. but was abandoned and resettled over the next 500 years. About 1500, Chucalissa's residents constructed large mounds, houses, and storage facilities around a central plaza where social and economic interaction took place. Archaeological excavations at Chucalissa, begun in the 1940s and 1950s, unearthed a Temple Mound where the Chief's House was constructed, as well as dwelling sites, burial mounds, skeletal remains, pottery, and artifacts. The Chief's House, a 50-square-foot structure built in the center of the mound, contained a large central hearth used for food preparation and subterranean storage pits where food and household utensils were stored. The floor was made of fired clay. Other houses in the village averaged 15 to 20 square feet. A mixture of mud and grass was used to cover the walls and native grasses to thatch the roof. In the 1500s, Chucalissa's residents hunted bear, deer, turkey, and small game with bows and arrows or fished from the Mississippi River or its tributaries for gar, carp, drum, or turtle. An artisan class made up of potters, weavers, and shaman enriched the cultural life of the community. Chucalissa's residents also traded surplus goods with neighboring villages.

Spain claimed much of the southern part of North America but did little to establish permanent settlements until the middle of the sixteenth century. In 1542, when Hernando De Soto arrived in what would eventually become Tennessee, he had already been in North America for three years. He had served as a captain in Francisco Pizarro's forces when the latter attacked the Incas of Peru in the 1530s. In 1539, in command of his own 600-man army, De Soto landed at Tampa Bay in Florida. He and his army marched through the Southeast before arriving in present-day Tennessee in 1540. Their relationships with Indians in the area were probably peaceful until they demanded food, information, and women from a group of Chiscas living near the upper Nolichucky River.

De Soto and his men were searching for gold and silver to rival what had been discovered by other Spanish conquistadors. Attracted by tales of prosperous native villages in the Mississippi River valley, De Soto's army arrived in the area of the Chickasaw Bluffs in 1542. They spent several weeks building rafts before crossing the river in early June at a point south of present-day Memphis and advancing north and west through Arkansas. After a winter of exploration and plunder, De Soto and his men began their return journey, probably along the Arkansas or the Red Rivers, down to the Mississippi. They occupied an Indian village called Guachoya where De Soto became ill and died on May 21, 1542. His body was weighed down with sand and thrown into the Mississippi River. The Native Americans were told that he had ascended into heaven.

In the two centuries following De Soto's visit, Indian cultures in the region of the Fourth Bluff declined in the face of disease and internal conflict. Spanish explorers brought smallpox, influenza, and measles for which the Indians had no natural immunity. The Spanish also attacked and ravaged native communities searching for gold and capturing slaves. Surviving communities relocated, split into smaller units, or formed confederacies like the northeastern Iroquois Confederation or the southeastern Five Civilized Tribes.

By the eighteenth century, the Chickasaws were the dominant tribe in the Mississippi Valley, but they faced a new set of European adventurers. French fur trappers, traders, and missionaries traveled from the valley of the St. Lawrence River through the Mississippi River Basin. In 1673, Father Jacques Marquette and fur trapper Louis Joliet traveled down the Mississippi River in a small canoe as far as the mouth of the Arkansas River in search of a route to the Pacific Ocean. They stopped at the Monsoupeleas or Mosopeleas Village of Agenatchi at one of the bluffs. Marquette wrote in his journal that the Indians "wear their hair long and mark their bodies in the Iroquois fashion; the head-dress and clothing of their women were like those of Huron squaws." Marquette described houses constructed by inhabitants on a system of elevated wooden grids. Underneath these grids they would place smudge pots and over them they hung animal pelts to combat the mosquitoes. The Indians served the two explorers a meal of buffalo meat and bears' oil with plums; but it was clear that the Frenchmen were not the first Europeans in the region since the Native Americans possessed guns, axes, hoes, knives, beads, and double-glass bottles.

Nine years after Marquette and Joliet visited Agenatchi, Robert Cavalier de La Salle passed by the Fourth Bluff on his journey to New Orleans. His journey was part of a French strategy to counter English and Spanish influence in North America by establishing a string of trading posts from the headwaters of the Mississippi River to the Gulf of Mexico. La Salle led a group of 54 Frenchmen and Indians to the area near the Chickasaw Bluffs. One of his men, Pierre Prudhomme, disappeared while hunting and La Salle constructed a small fort, Fort Prudhomme, as a temporary base while the group searched for the man. Prudhomme returned two days later and La Salle and his men continued their journey south. But before he left the region, La Salle named a small river near the Fourth Bluff after a Loup Indian, Mayot, who accompanied his party. Riviere a Mayot became the Riviere du Loup; the name was eventually translated to the Wolf River. La Salle's brother, Abbe Jean Cavalier, wrote the first description of what he called the "Chickasaw Bluffs." He described them as "precipices rising to a height of eighty to a hundred feet; all of different colored earths" and extending for a "league and a half" (about 4.5 miles) on the right side of the river.

As in other parts of North America, relationships between the French and Native Americans along the Mississippi River were relatively peaceful. France's agricultural settlements were clustered along the St. Lawrence River and, unlike English, Dutch, and other foreign colonists, the French *coureurs de bois* (runners of the woods) were more concerned with trade than with permanent settlement. They needed the Indians to help supply a growing European market for furs. However, conflicts in Europe from the late seventeenth century through the middle of the eighteenth century had serious implications for all European colonists and Indians.

From 1688 until 1763, European nations were involved in a series of wars for world domination. Most of the fighting occurred in Europe, but some conflicts spilled over to European colonies throughout the world, including North America. English and French armies and their respective Indian allies battled in the Native American territory between New England and New France.

In the Treaty of Utrecht, which ended the third war (the War of the Spanish Succession or Queen Anne's War), Louis XIV placed his grandson on the Spanish throne as King Philip V of Spain, but the Spanish and French thrones were to remain permanently separate. More important for colonial North America, some French territory in Canada, including Arcadia (renamed Nova Scotia), was ceded to the British.

Despite the territorial losses, France tried, with little success, to strengthen her colonial presence by reinforcing the forts in the Mississippi Valley. In 1729, a group of Natchez Indians massacred a French garrison at Fort Rosalie in retaliation for brutal treatment of the Indians by the French. The French responded by nearly wiping out the Natchez Indians. The few survivors conveyed their intense hatred of the French to the Chickasaw bands they joined, and this enmity soon affected life in the region. Seven years after the Fort Rosalie massacre, when Jean Baptiste Le Moyne, Sieur de Bienville, traveled up the Tombignee River from New Orleans to join another French army coming down river, the Chickasaws defeated each army before they could unite. In 1739, Bienville again tried to reassert French control over the region by constructing Fort Assumption at the Fourth Bluff as a base from which his 3,500-man army of Frenchmen and Indians could lead attacks on neighboring Chickasaw towns. But Bienville's army, weakened by disease and desertion, was forced to abandon the fort and return to New Orleans.

Like much of the American continent, the Fourth Bluff was caught up in the global tussles between England, France, and Spain for power. The struggle in the American colonies came to a head with the French and Indian War (1754-1763). Unlike the three preceding conflicts, the French and Indian War began with clashes between French troops and militia from Virginia in the Ohio Valley and spread to the European continent. In the aftermath of this war, a victorious England claimed all French territories east of the Mississippi River, but control of the river and France's western territories went to Spain. Britain now faced the problem of governing her far-flung empire with a depleted treasury. The continuing discord between settlers and Indians were among Britain's most pressing problems in the Americas. The Proclamation of 1763, which prohibited migration west of the Appalachian Mountains, was designed to make it easier for Britain to manage relations in the new western territories, but to Americans who had fought to wrest these territories from the French, England's actions seemed repressive and tyrannical. Besides, it was a proclamation impossible to enforce. Britain's armies were spread thinly throughout America's coastal settlements, leaving colonists free to move around in the territories west of the Proclamation Line.

***

In 1763, the Chickasaws controlled the Fourth Bluff, but they used the area primarily as hunting grounds and as a trading site. Weakened by warfare with the French and by exposure to Old World diseases, they hoped for peaceful relationships with the British. The English had little time or money to spend on Indian problems in the west. Despite the terms of the Proclamation of 1763, American migration west of the Appalachian Mountains went virtually unchecked in the three decades following the ouster of the French and the transfer of their Louisiana territory to British and Spanish control. The Spanish established the northern boundary of their territory on the east bank of the Mississippi River at the Yazoo River and conceded the territory north of this point to the British. In 1766, Englishman Thomas Hutchins visited the Fourth Bluff and noted its prospects as a "commanding, airy, pleasant, and extensive situation for settlements." Hutchins was probably the first European to think of the Fourth Bluffs a site for a permanent town.

During the Revolutionary War, although officially loyal to their British allies, the Chickasaws were also allied with individual American rebels such as James Robertson of Nashville. Americans negotiated for the right to construct forts in Chickasaw territory, and the tribe focused their anger on the Spanish who controlled the Mississippi River and the Louisiana Territory. From their sanctuary on the Wolf River, Chickasaw raiding parties, led by James Logan Colbert, the Scotsman who was their chief, attacked Spanish vessels. Colbert was married to three Chickasaw sisters and his sons William (Chooshemataha), George (Tootmastubbe), Levi (Itawamba), and James (no Indian name is recorded for this fourth son), were prominent figures in relations between the tribe and Americans in the nineteenth century.

When the Revolutionary War ended, the Chickasaws transferred their political allegiance from Britain to the new American nation, but relations at the Fourth Bluff remained unsettled into the next decade. The Fourth Bluff was the focus of a three-way power struggle between the Chickasaws, the Americans, and the Spanish. As American farmers moved into the Old Southwest, the Mississippi River was an increasingly important transportation artery for Midwestern and mid-Southern farmers and traders. Spanish control of the river restricted the ability of American farmers to fully exploit the region. National leaders continually renegotiated with Spain for the right to navigate the Mississippi, but not to the satisfaction of either nation. Like the French before them, American settlers decided to construct a fort at the Fourth Bluff to limit Spanish influence. The fort would also encourage trade through Nashville rather than the Spanish cities of Pensacola and Mobile. But the Spanish decided to resolve the conflict by declaring the Chickasaw nation a Spanish dependency and constructing fortifications at the Fourth Bluff from which they could govern the region.

In 1795, the Spanish sent Dom Manuel Gayoso de Lemos, governor of the Natchez district, to purchase land from the Chickasaws and establish a garrison at the Wolf and Mississippi Rivers. Gayoso, with the assistance of Benjamin Fooy, a Dutch immigrant who had lived within the tribe in the 1780s, negotiated with pro-Spanish Chickasaw leader Ugulayacabe for the site. Gayoso brought in artillery and raised the Spanish flag at Fort San Fernando de las Barrancas, or St. Ferdinand of the Bluffs, on May 30, 1795. He considered the fort an extension of his river fleet of three barges (*La Felipa*, *La Flecha*, and *El Rayo*) that were anchored nearby.

Bounded by Bayou Gayoso, the Wolf River, the Mississippi River, and Nonconnah Creek, the fort was situated on a point that was militarily indefensible. It was at the first high ground beyond Bayou Gayoso, but was surrounded on the east and south by higher ground that might be occupied by an enemy force. The view upriver was also obstructed by an island at the mouth of the Wolf River. Garrisoned by a force of over 125 men and with eight 8-pounders as artillery, Fort San Fernando had a central square that was 200 feet on each side, with diagonal bastions extending another 75 feet at each corner. The commander's residence, barracks for the men, and a tile-covered powder magazine were located inside the stockade. South of the fort was a large building with gardens, a hospital, and a "habitation" (possibly belonging to Benjamin Fooy) with more formal gardens. Near these buildings was the trading post and warehouse of Panton, Leslie, and Company from Mobile. Although it appeared to be carefully conceived and laid out, Fort Gayoso was a difficult post for the Spanish soldiers garrisoned there. In two years of occupation, the fort had four commandants. The jail was usually full, disease was rampant, medical care was unsatisfactory, and food supplies were inadequate. Since there was no lime to make mortar, the military contingent could not construct ovens to bake bread.

Pro-American chief Piomingo and James Colbert's son William (Chooshemataha) led the Chickasaw opposition to the Spanish fort. However, Spanish occupation of the Fourth Bluff and Fort San Fernando was short lived, not so much because of Piomingo's opposition as international relations. Five months after it was completed, Thomas Pinckney, U.S. minister to Great Britain, negotiated a treaty with Spain settling the southern and western boundaries of the United States at the 31st parallel and the Mississippi River. Pinckney's Treaty also recognized the right of United States citizens to navigate the Mississippi River and the right of deposit and transshipment from the port of New Orleans. Spain occupied Fort San Fernando until March 1797, then dismantled the stockade and took some of the logs across the Mississippi River and constructed a smaller fortification at Esperanza, Arkansas. Benjamin Fooy moved his business to this site where he constructed a "vast and handsome residence." But when the city of Memphis was laid out in 1819, Fooy returned to the Fourth Bluff and was given a lot near the site of the house he had occupied at Fort San Fernando.

Spain's influence in the Mississippi Valley ended at the beginning of the nineteenth century. In 1800, they transferred control of the Mississippi River, the Louisiana Territory, and the port of New Orleans back to the

French in the Treaty of San Ildefonso. The U.S. government was not immediately aware of the transfer of the Louisiana Territory since Spanish governors continued to serve in New Orleans for several years. However, when French control of the Louisiana Territory and the port of New Orleans became a reality, President Thomas Jefferson authorized a delegation to offer a maximum of $10 million for the port city. Napoleon, faced with war in Europe and difficulty suppressing rebellions on the Caribbean island of Saint-Domingue (Haiti), decided to sell the entire Louisiana Territory to the United States for $15 million.

Benjamin Fooy warned the Chickasaws that the withdrawal of the Spanish from Fort San Fernando in 1797 would not end their troubles with white settlers; and the Louisiana Purchase marked the beginning of the end of Chickasaw influence at the Fourth Bluff. The tribe was anxious to trade with the Americans for weapons to make war on their enemies, the Creeks, but Americans were as anxious to acquire land as trading rights. The strategic location of the Fourth Bluff was as apparent to the U.S. government as it had been to France, England, and Spain. While visitors to western Tennessee in the late eighteenth century commented on the regal demeanor of the Chickasaws, (English traveler Francis Baily, who visited the area in May 1797, described them as a "well-made, handsome race of men" who welcomed their visitors with "a pipe of peace") they also remarked on the suitability of the Fourth Bluff as a permanent American settlement.

About four months after the Spanish abandoned Fort San Fernando in March 1797, American army Captain Isaac Guion arrived at the Fourth Bluff en route to his post in Natchez. Guion established Fort Adams, named for President John Adams, at the site of the abandoned Spanish fort. The next commandants of Fort Adams were Lieutenant Joseph Campbell and Captain John Pierce (he died a few months after he assumed command of the post). Captain Meriwether Lewis (leader of the Lewis and Clark expedition in 1804-1806), also remained for only a few months. Soon after Lewis left, Fort Adams was abandoned and Fort Pickering, named for then Secretary of State Timothy Pickering, was established 2 miles south of the site. Captain Zebulon Pike, father of the noted nineteenth century explorer Zebulon M. Pike, became commander of Fort Pickering in October 1800. Pike remained at the fort for nine years before he was replaced by Lieutenant Zachary Taylor (who, 40 years later, became the twelfth president of the United States). Meriwether Lewis revisited the fort in 1809, and stayed for a few weeks recovering from a serious illness. Lewis, seemingly recovered, left for Washington but was killed or committed suicide on the Natchez Trace.

Fort Pickering served as a "factory" for exchanging pelts and furs brought in by Indian trappers for supplies. The factory system was intended to pull the Indians deeper into debt so that they would be forced to exchange their eastern lands for areas west of the Mississippi River. Early factors included Thomas Peterkin, Peter Morgan, David Hogg, and Robert Bayly. Benjamin Fooy returned to the Fourth Bluff as factor following Bayly's untimely death and was succeeded in 1814 by the most prominent of the nineteenth-century factors, Isaac Rawlings. Rawlings was born in Calvert County, Maryland in 1788, the son of a physician and grandson of a member of the Committee of Safety during the Revolutionary War. Rawlings remained as factor of Fort Pickering until 1816, when he was assigned to set up a new factory for Cherokee Indians who had moved to the Arkansas River. He returned to the Fourth Bluff in the early 1820s and was a leading figure in the development of the city of Memphis.

By the early 1800s, conditions at Fort Pickering had deteriorated. One observer commented that "The post of Chickasaw Bluffs is represented to be unhealthy. What objection can there be to remove, during the summer, the Garrison, leaving a subaltern of discretion with a few men." Other factors complained about the "lawless vending of whiskey and the insolence of the Indians in the absence of a Garrison." The last American troops probably left Fort Pickering in 1813, and the factory system ended in 1822. In 1818, the Chickasaw cession of the northern portion of their lands to the federal government opened the way for more American settlers at the Fourth Bluff. Within ten years the city of Memphis and the county of Shelby were surveyed, laid out, and chartered. What had been an economically and militarily strategic location for Native-American and foreign powers continued to be one of the most important sites on the Mississippi River between St. Louis and New Orleans.

British claims to the Chickasaw Bluffs had been based on the loose boundaries Elizabeth I had assigned to Sir Walter Raleigh's doomed Virginia colony and on Charles II's charter for the Carolina colonies. This charter granted colonial proprietors "title" to lands extending westward from the Atlantic to the Pacific Ocean. After the Revolutionary War, North Carolina claimed the territory from its western boundary to the Mississippi River.

The state ceded its claims to the federal government in 1790, but not before dispensing generous land grants to Revolutionary War veterans or selling land to pay war debts. Some of these land sales or grants included territory belonging to the Chickasaws. In October 1783, the land speculators who controlled North Carolina's government opened the Chickasaw lands to purchase. More scrupulous legislators ended the practice seven months later, but by then more than half of what was later to become the Western District of Tennessee had been claimed by speculators.

Among the early claimants were John Rice and John Ramsey, who bought title to two adjoining 5,000-acre tracts of land on the Fourth Bluff. These early claimants paid about 5¢ an acre for what would eventually become the heart of downtown Memphis. In 1791, John Rice was killed by Indians near Clarksville, about 10 miles from the Tennessee-Kentucky border. The Rice estate passed to his heirs who eventually sold the Fourth Bluff tract to John Overton and Andrew Jackson. Tennessee became a state on June 1, 1796. The following year, Jackson sold part of his share to Stephen and Richard Winchester for $625. The two made a quick profit by selling the claim to their brothers, James and William, for $1,000. The original Rice tract now belonged to John Overton (one-half), Andrew Jackson (one-fourth), and William and James Winchester (one-fourth jointly). William Winchester died in 1812, and after the Chickasaw land cession in 1818, Jackson eventually sold another portion to James Winchester for $5,000. An acre of land that cost Rice 5¢ in the 1790s, was now worth $8. The Fourth Bluff, originally part of Washington County, North Carolina, became a part of the state of Tennessee on June 1, 1796, after a census indicated that the population had reached 77,000.

In the second decade of the nineteenth century, there was pressure to open even more Chickasaw land to white settlement. The Tennessee legislature petitioned Congress to relinquish the Chickasaw claim and Congress created a special commission to deal with them. General Jackson was appointed to represent Tennessee and ex-Governor Isaac Shelby to represent Kentucky since the tribe had lands in both states.

The Chickasaws, who at first refused to meet with the commissioners, gave in to pressure from Jackson and Shelby and joined in a council at the Chickasaw Old Town site near Aberdeen, Mississippi, in the fall of 1818. The American representatives gained concessions from the Native Americans by intimidation and threats. The Indians agreed to move below the Tennessee-Mississippi border in exchange for $300,000, to be paid in 15 annual installments. The Chickasaws ceded about 6,848,000 acres at approximately 4.5¢ per acre. Surveyors for the presidential commission established the Tennessee's southern boundary with Mississippi and made the Chickasaw Bluffs part of the western boundary. When representatives Levi Colbert and Captain Seely of the Chickasaw Nation, who were part of the commission, complained that surveyors' southern boundary line cut too deeply into the Chickasaw lands, James Winchester, the head of the commission and a proprietary partner in the Rice tract, explained that the instruments used to mark off the land were "more accurate than the path of the sun." Colbert and Seely were not satisfied and left the party to confer with tribal leaders. They later met with Winchester at the Fourth Bluff after he completed the survey. Colbert and Seely declared the line was inaccurate and asked for a resurvey. The Chickasaw Nation lodged a formal protest and worked for ten years to get the boundaries changed.

Protests may have developed when the Chickasaws realized they were giving up the Fourth Bluff. They had no towns or religious shrines in the area, and there were no salt springs or natural resources nearby, but the Fourth Bluff had been an important trading site for centuries. In reality, the Cession line was actually too far north, giving the Chickasaws 440 square miles more than they were entitled to in the treaty. The boundary line was corrected in 1837, after the state of Mississippi had taken title to the rest of the Chickasaw lands.

In 1819, James Winchester recommended that a new county be established in western Tennessee. It was laid out as a rectangle, 30 miles wide by 25 miles long, with the Mississippi River as its western boundary. Winchester, Overton, and Jackson also met at Jackson's Nashville home, the Hermitage, to discuss plans for a new town at the Fourth Bluff. It included 362 lots, broad avenues, four public squares, and a public promenade along the waterfront. Winchester suggested the town be named Memphis. His familiarity with the classics was evidenced in the names he chose for his own children, Marcus, Brutus, Selina, Lucilius, Almire, Napoleon, and Valerius Publicola. Although other American towns were named for the ancient cities—Athens, Rome, Catharge, Corinth—few were named for cities in ancient Egypt. Winchester considered the Mississippi River the American Nile and hoped Memphis on the Mississippi would become a center for trade and culture just as Memphis on the Nile had been. The proprietors ordered maps engraved and took out ads in newspapers advertising their real estate venture. James Winchester's son Marcus and William Lawrence were sent to the Bluff to survey and lay out the town. They completed their work in May 1819, and the first lots were sold to settlers who were already in residence at the site.

Five months later, John Overton petitioned the state legislature for the formation of Shelby County and some county officers were chosen. By the spring of 1820, there were more than 50 people living within the new county of Shelby. At the Fourth Bluff, James Winchester gave his son Marcus a large tract (bordered now by Manassas, Poplar, McNeil, and Union) where the younger Winchester and Anderson Carr built a store. John Overton encouraged settlement and trade by giving lots to other businessmen for a tavern, a mill, and a tannery. But when other lots were put up for public sale in December 1820, the results were disappointing.

In 1823, Andrew Jackson traded his interest in the Memphis site to John C. McLemore, who was married to Rachel Jackson's niece Elizabeth Donelson, for a tract of land in Madison County. McLemore tried to develop Memphis for the next five years before moving on to another real estate project, the creation of the neighboring town of Fort Pickering, on land he had purchased south of Memphis. Fort Pickering included an Indian trading post, a boat works, factories, a candy plant, and a brewery. It also had a newspaper called the *Eagle* and a boarding school for girls.

Memphis was incorporated by the state of Tennessee on December 9, 1826, over the opposition of some early settlers like Isaac Rawlings, who thought the city had not developed enough wealth or population to need a town government and that supporting a government would be too costly for the poor living in the outskirts of town. Marcus Winchester countered by arguing that incorporation was essential for the town's growth, and proposed that town leaders simply leave the poor in the outskirts. Within two years of incorporation, Rawlings had come on board as a leading proponent of city government. In March 1827, citizens elected the first aldermen: Marcus Winchester, Joseph L. Davis, John Hooke, N.B. Atwood, George F. Graham, John R. Dougherty, and William D. Neely. At their first meeting they chose Winchester as mayor, Rawlings as treasurer, Jacob L. Davis as recorder, and John J. Balch as town constable. The aldermen also passed the town's first ordinances including taxes on lots, all free males between the ages of 21 and 50, all slaves between the ages of 12 and 50, wholesale and retail stores, professionals, tavern keepers, retailers of alcoholic beverages and "stud horses and jacks." The town limits in 1826 were fixed as follows:

> Beginning at the intersection of Wolf River with the Mississippi River; thence with Wolf River to the mouth of Bayou Gayoso; thence with said bayou to the county bridge; thence with the line of the second alley east of, and parallel with Second street to Union street; thence at right angle to Second street to the western boundary of the tract of land entered to John Rice by the grant number 283, dated April 25, 1789; thence with the said western boundary up the Mississippi River to the Wolf River.

In 1828, the original proprietors (Overton, Winchester, and McLemore) gave the city Auction, Market, Exchange, and Court Squares and the waterfront promenade as public grounds. The original charter was amended in 1828, giving the town the same powers as Nashville but providing that the mayor could not hold any office under the federal government. This meant Winchester, who was serving as postmaster, could not be reelected mayor.

Despite the efforts of early settlers and proprietors to encourage the development of Memphis as an economic and political center for southwestern Tennessee, the city faced intense competition from several rivals. Even the state legislature seemed to be working against the town's advancement. When Shelby County was incorporated in 1824, a commission chose a site in the center of the Shelby County at Sanderlin's Bluff, rather than Memphis, as the county seat. The town of Raleigh was then laid out at that site on 29 acres of land purchased from Wilson Sanderlin and 22 acres bought from James Freeman. In 1827, the first court session was held in a newly constructed courthouse. Raleigh became a bustling town and businesses like the Union Inn operated to meet the needs of the permanent and transient population. In 1829, a school for boys opened and was followed eight years later by the Raleigh Female Academy. The original frame courthouse was replaced in the mid-1830s with a two-story brick building.

By the late 1830s, however, Memphis began to surpass Raleigh in economic and political importance. Courts began meeting in Memphis to deal with the criminal element in the growing riverboat town and, as the population increased in the 1840s and 1850s, other judicial and legislative proceedings were organized in the city. It was clear by 1860 that Memphis, not Raleigh, was the political center of Shelby County, a fact supported by the decision to move the county seat to the city. But the Civil War prevented the removal of the government until 1866.

In addition to Fort Pickering and Raleigh, Memphis also contended with the town of Randolph for economic influence during this early period. Randolph was located about 50 miles upriver from Memphis in neighboring Tipton County. It was on the second Chickasaw Bluff at the lower mouth of the Hatchie River, the largest of the four rivers draining west Tennessee into the Mississippi River. Steamboats could travel up the Hatchie as far as Bolivar, Tennessee, and Randolph had a good landing for flatboats. Although Randolph was established after Memphis, by 1829 it had three warehouses, six dry-goods stores, ten physicians, one tavern, and twenty or thirty families. Five years later, New Yorker Francis Latham was publishing a newspaper, the *Randolph Recorder*, and in the 1830s the town had four hotels, nearly fifty businesses, and several private schools, including a college. However, Randolph declined in the late 1830s as a result of several economic and political blows. First, the state legislature chose another town as the county seat for Tipton County. Then a mail line, established in 1829 from Nashville to Memphis, bypassed Randolph and a dispute developed over ownership of the town. Finally, in 1835, a military road was constructed linking Memphis to Little Rock. Randolph's citizens had proposed a canal to connect the Hatchie with the Tennessee River, but Andrew Jackson's opposition to federal support for internal improvements doomed this plan and eventually the city.

***

The growth of Memphis as a major economic and political center for the upper Mississippi Valley was tied to cotton, slavery, and to developments in transportation. By the 1830s, cotton cultivation was firmly established in the region. Wagons and small boats brought bales of the fiber to Memphis to be transported to markets downriver and eventually to textile mills in the Northeast and Europe. By the 1850s, Memphis was the "Biggest Inland Cotton Market in the World." On the eve of the Civil War, almost 400,000 bales of cotton left the city's wharves each year.

The expansion of cotton merchandising in Memphis was closely tied to the expansion of slavery in western Tennessee and the Mississippi Delta. In Shelby County, the slave population increased from 103 in 1820 to 16,953 in 1860, when slaves made up just over one-third of the county's total population. Most of this increase was in rural areas outside Memphis. Some farmers and planters had only one or two slaves while others owned hundreds. Even those who owned only a few laborers were invested in the system since they could hire more slave laborers when necessary. In 1860, enslaved African Americans made up 17 percent of Memphis' population. Most worked as mechanics, draymen, assistants to some craftsmen, cooks, washerwomen, and domestic servants.

Slave trading was an important part of the city's economy. One of the best known firms was that of Byrd Hill and Nathan Bedford Forrest. Hill and Forrest and other slave trading establishments like Bolton and Dickens, Zach Curlin, W.E. Eliot, and M.C. Cayce made Memphis the largest slave trading center of any city in the mid-South. Although Tennessee laws prohibited auctions like those common in other slaveholding states, slaves were sold from offices and yards in such frequency that by the 1850s, Memphis was the biggest inland slave market in the South.

CHAPTER THREE

THE BATTLE FOR MEMPHIS

Shelby Foote

Hoax or no, the Confederate retrograde movement was, after all, a retreat; and as such it had its consequences. Fort Pillow, being completely outflanked, was evacuated June 4, along with the supplementary Fort Randolph, fifteen miles below. Now all that stood between the Federal ironclads and Memphis was the eight-boat flotilla which had been resting on its laurels since the affair at Plum Run Bend. Captain Montgomery had said then that the Yankees would "never penetrate farther down" unless their fleet was reinforced; but two days after Pillow and Randolph were abandoned he discovered, in the most shocking way, that it had indeed been reinforced.

Back in March — after years of failing to interest the navy in his theory — an elderly civil engineer named Charles Ellet, Jr., wrote and sent to the War Department a pamphlet applying the formula $f = mv^2$ to demonstrate the superiority of the ram as a naval weapon, particularly in river engagements, which allowed scant room for dodging. Stanton read it and reacted. He sent for the author, made him a colonel, and told him to build as many of the rams as he thought would be needed to knock the rebels off the Mississippi. Ellet got to work at once, purchasing and converting suitable steamers, and joined the ironclad fleet above Fort Pillow on May 25 with nine of the strange-looking craft. They carried neither guns nor armor, since neither had any place in the mass-velocity formula; nor did they have sharp dogtooth prows, which Ellet said would plug a hole as quickly as they punched one. All his dependence was on the two formula-components. Velocity was assured by installing engines designed to yield a top speed of fifteen knots, which would make them the fastest things on the river, and "mass" was attained by packing the bows with lumber and running three solid bulkheads, a foot or more in thickness, down the length of each vessel, so that the impact of the whole rigid unit would be delivered at a single stroke. Engines and boilers were braced for the shock of ramming, and the crews were river men whose courage Ellet tested in various ways, getting rid of many in the process. Perhaps his greatest caution, however, was shown in the selection of his captains. All were Pennsylvanians, like himself, and all were named Ellet. Seven were brothers and nephews of the designer-commander, and the eighth was his nineteen-year-old son.

Anxious to put $f = mv^2$ to work, the thin-faced lank-haired colonel was for going down and pitching into the rebel flotilla as soon as he joined up, but Flag Officer Davis had learned caution at Plum Run Bend. In spite of the fact that both sunken ironclads had been raised from their shallow graves and put back into service, the fleet was still under strength, three of its seven units having returned to Cairo for repairs. No matter, Ellet said; he and his kinsmen were still for immediate action, with or without the ironclads. But Davis continued to refuse the "concurrence" Stanton had told the colonel he would have to have in working with the navy.

The Confederates in Memphis, knowing nothing of all this, had assumed from reports that the new arrivers were some kind of transport. They relied on the guns of Forts Pillow and Randolph; or if the batteries failed to stop the Yankees, there was still the eight-boat flotilla which had given them such a drubbing three weeks back. Moreover, as at New Orleans, the keels of two monster ironclads, the *Arkansas* and the *Tennessee*, had been laid in the city's yards. The former, having been launched and armored up to her maindeck, was floated down to Vicksburg, then towed up the Yazoo River for completion in safety after the fall of Island Ten; but the latter was still on the stocks, awaiting the arrival of her armor. Like the city itself, she would have to take her chances that the enemy would be stopped.

Those chances were considerably thinned by the evacuation of Corinth and the two forts upriver. It now became a question of which would get there first, a sizeable portion of Halleck's Grand Army or the Federal fleet. The citizens hoped it would be the latter, for they had the gunboat flotilla to stand in its way, while there was absolutely nothing at all to stand in the way of the former. They got their wish. At dawn of June 6, two days after Fort Pillow was abandoned, the ironclads showed up, coming round the bend called Paddy's Hen and Chickens, four of them in line abreast just above the city, offering battle to the eight Confederate gunboats. The people turned out in tens of thousands, lining the bluffs for a grandstand seat at what they hoped would be a reenactment of the affair at Plum Run Bend. The first shot was fired at sunup, and they cheered and waved their handkerchiefs as at a tableau when the southern gunboats, mounting 28 light cannon, moved out to meet their squat black bug-shaped northern opponents, mounting 68, mostly heavy.

Ellet had his rams in rear of the ironclad line of battle. When the first shot was fired, he took off his hat and waved it to attract the attention of his brother commanding the ram alongside his own. "Round out and follow me! Now is our chance!" he cried. Both boats sprang forward under full heads of steam and knifed between the ironclads, whose crews gave them a cheer as they went by. Ellet made straight for the *Colonel Lovell*, leader of the Confederate line, and when she swerved at the last minute to avoid a head-on collision, struck her broadside and cut her almost in two. She sank within a few minutes: brief, conclusive proof of the relation between force and mv^2. Meanwhile his brother had accomplished something different. Striking for the *General Price*, which held her course while the General Beauregard moved to aid her by converging on the ram, he darted between the two — which then collided in his wake. The *General Price* lost one of her sidewheels, sheared off in the crash, and while she limped toward bank, out of the fight, the ram came about in a long swift curve and rammed the *Beauregard* at the moment the rebel's steam drum was punctured by a shell from one of the ironclads. She struck her colors.

Four of the remaining five did not last much longer, and none ever managed to come to grips with an adversary. Montgomery's *Little Rebel*, the only screw steamer of the lot, took a shell in her machinery, then went staggering into the Arkansas bank, where her crew made off through the woods. The *Jeff Thompson* was set afire by a Federal broadside; the *Sumter* and the *Bragg*, like the flagship, were knocked into bank by the Dahlgrens. The whole engagement lasted no longer than the one at Plum Run Bend, which it avenged. One Confederate was sunk beyond raising; two were burned; four were captured, and in time became part of the fleet they had fought. Van Dorn, the only survivor, managed to get enough of a head start in the confusion to make a getaway downriver. Two of the rams gave chase for a while, but then turned back to join the celebration.

The cheering was all on the river, where the rams and ironclads anchored unopposed, not on the bluffs, where the cheers had turned to groans. Smoke had blanketed the water; all the spectators could see was the flash of Union guns and the tall paired stacks of Confederate steamboats riding above the murk. Pair by pair, in rapid order, the crown-top chimneys disappeared. "The deep sympathizing wail which followed each disaster," one who heard it wrote, "went up like a funeral dirge from the assembled multitude, and had an overwhelming pathos." When the sun-dazzled smoke finally cleared away they saw that their flotilla had been not only defeated but abolished, and they turned sadly away to await the occupation which the Corinth retreat had made inevitable anyhow. There still was time to burn the *Tennessee*, sitting armorless on the stocks, and this they did, taking considerable satisfaction in at least making sure that she would never be part of the fleet whose destruction had been the aim of her designers. It was bitter, however, to surrender as they did to a nineteen-year-old medical cadet, Colonel Ellet's son, who landed in a rowboat with three seamen and a folded flag, the stars and stripes, which presently he was hoisting over the post office. Later that day the two regiments Pope had left behind marched in for the formal occupation. Thus was Memphis returned to her old allegiance.

Colonel Ellet himself did not come ashore. The only Federal casualty of the engagement, he had been pinked in the knee by a pistol ball while waving his hat on the hurricane deck of his flagship, directing the ram attack. The wound, though painful, was not considered dangerous; prone on the deck, he continued in command throughout the fight; but infection set in, and he died of it two weeks later, while being taken north aboard one of the rams. Before his death, however, he had the satisfaction of proving his theory in action and of knowing that his genius — in conjunction with the no doubt larger genius of that other civil engineer, James Eads — had cleared the Mississippi down to Vicksburg, whose batteries now would be grist for Davis' and Farragut's upper and nether millstones.

CHAPTER FOUR

THE CIVIL WAR AND ITS LEGACY IN MEMPHIS

Timothy S. Huebner

While the vast majority of the American Civil War played out on southern soil, Memphis was one of the few cities in the Confederacy that suffered no physical destruction. As a river city in the Western Theater of the conflict, where Union success came relatively quickly during the first two years of the war, Memphis fell on June 6, 1862, after a brief clash of Union and Confederate vessels on the Mississippi River. Passing unscathed into Union hands that day, Memphis acquired few battle scars. Nevertheless, the subsequent wartime experience of the city deeply affected its character, both culturally and demographically. For the next four years, federal forces occupied the city while freedom-seeking African Americans sought refuge there. These two inextricably connected events—Union occupation and Black in-migration—left a lasting impression. If unchanged by the Battle of Memphis on the surface, the Bluff City was nevertheless profoundly transformed by the Civil War.[1]

Viewed from the perspective of Memphis' unique environmental and social history, the Civil War's origins were deep and long. Centuries of flooding in the Lower Mississippi Valley transported layer upon layer of topsoil onto decomposing vegetation in a thousand-mile-long geographic expanse stretching from Cairo, Illinois, to New Orleans. In the middle of this vast flood plain stood a handful of bluffs in what eventually became the southwest corner of the state of Tennessee. Memphis, laid out on the southernmost of these bluffs in 1819, was thus favorably situated on high ground in the middle of the flood plain of a great river. The city grew slowly at first, as rough, transient flatboat men gave the outpost a reputation for lawlessness during its first two decades. Not until the 1840s with the rise of steamboats and a stable municipal government did its population experience rapid growth.[2]

The city's position at the head of the Yazoo-Mississippi Delta, an especially fertile portion of the Lower Mississippi Valley, shaped its antebellum identity. White planters, who had migrated into the wilds of the Delta beginning in the 1830s, brought enslaved Black laborers to clear the land and plant cotton. Within a few decades the Bluff City became inextricably linked to the region as a center for the cotton trade—a place where bales were classed, priced, sold, and shipped. Growing global demand for cotton reinforced the desire for slave labor, and between 1820 and 1860 approximately 875,000 Black men, women, and children were transported between the Upper South and Deep South as part of the domestic slave trade. Many ended up in the Delta.[3] Memphis became a regional hub for this traffic in humans, with Adams Street at the locus of this trade. Located in the heart of town and connecting the riverfront steamboat landing to the Memphis and Charleston Railroad line, the street offered easy access to buyers and sellers. By 1860, six of the ten slave dealerships in the city— including the leading firm, owned by Nathan Bedford Forrest—were located along Adams. While enslaved people constituted only 17% of the city's residents in 1860, Memphis found itself increasingly connected, like the rest of the Deep South, to plantation agriculture and the institution of slavery that sustained it.[4]

Commitment to slavery ultimately manifested itself in secession. Cautious in their initial response to the 1860 election of Republican Abraham Lincoln as president, Memphians came to favor disunion, like most of the rest of the state of Tennessee, after the Civil War began and Lincoln called for troops to put down the southern rebellion. The city's mayor, John Park, stated in his inaugural address in July 1861 that, if the state remained in the Union, it faced a dire future. Park portrayed Lincoln and the Republicans as representing "a fanatical party" that focused on "combining republicanism, abolitionism, free-loveism, atheism, with every other abominable ism that strikes at the organization of society or the existence of free constitutional government." Confronted with a party that, in his mind, threatened to undermine slavery and the entire social order, Park argued that the South had "no alternative" but to secede.[5] Memphians thus supported the state's June 8, 1861, referendum on secession, which ratified the decision of the legislature to leave the Union.

Once the war began, the Lower Mississippi Valley became central to the Union strategy in the western theater of the conflict. While Confederate President Jefferson Davis concentrated most of his military assets in the eastern theater, where Stonewall Jackson and eventually Robert E. Lee developed an aura of invincibility, the Confederate West suffered a different fate. There Union General Ulysses S. Grant won early victories at Forts

Henry and Donelson in the northwestern part of Tennessee, triumphs that secured river routes into the Confederacy and led to the Union occupation of Nashville. These Union successes prompted the Confederates, under the command of Gen. Albert Sydney Johnston, to give up much of Tennessee and retreat to Corinth, a key railroad junction in northern Mississippi. In April 1862, Johnston's army launched an unsuccessful attempt to beat back Grant's forces, who had camped just across the Tennessee state line near a small steamboat landing. Defeat at the Battle of Shiloh, a bloody two-day affair, prompted the Confederates to again retreat to Corinth. Meanwhile, the very next day, Confederates surrendered to Gen. John Pope's forces at Island Number Ten, a two-mile wide island in the Mississippi River near the Kentucky-Tennessee line and the only stronghold protecting the lower Mississippi. Defeated on land and water in the region surrounding Memphis, Rebel forces all but left the city for the taking.[6]

After securing Fort Pillow, located downriver from Island Number Ten, the Union's "brown-water navy," steamed toward Memphis. At dawn on June 6, five Union ironclad gunboats and two rams—light, unarmed vessels intended to smash enemy ships—met the eight vessels of the Confederate River Defense Fleet. Thousands of local civilian residents lined the bluff to cheer on the Confederate ships, the decks of which were stacked high with bales of cotton, rather than iron, for protection. The onlookers were soon disappointed. In the hour-and-a-half battle that ensued, the Union sank or destroyed all but one Confederate vessel. The attack by the rams, under the command of Colonel Charles Ellet, Jr., an engineer who had developed the ram fleet at the direction of the War Department, proved "bold and successful."[7] Wounded in the battle, Ellet was the only Union casualty that day, compared to 180 men on the Confederate side. After the battle, Union Flag Officer Charles H. Davis demanded the surrender of the city, and Mayor Park, admitting that it had "no resources of defense," acknowledged to Flag Officer Davis, "the city is in your power." That day Union forces raised the U.S. flag over the post office building.[8] The fall of Memphis marked a significant strategic victory for the Union in the West, for it came less than two months after New Orleans and Baton Rouge had suffered similar fates, leaving Vicksburg as the only remaining Confederate outpost on the Mississippi River.

Much to the chagrin of local Whites, for the rest of the war Memphis was a federally-occupied city. Thousands of Confederate-sympathizing

Memphians fled, but those who stayed behind seemed intent on disrupting the occupation. When Grant arrived in town on June 23, he reported "great disloyalty manifested by the citizens of this place," and his immediate successor, Gen. Alvin P. Hovey, ordered that all male residents between the ages of eighteen and forty-five be required to take an oath of allegiance to the United States or face banishment. [9] Gen. William T. Sherman, who replaced Hovey and stayed in the city for four months, announced his intention to enforce the order, but loyalty, Sherman learned, could neither be imposed nor cultivated. Defiance took many forms. Parishioners at Calvary Episcopal Church, for example, omitted the president of the United States in their Sunday morning petitions. In attendance one Sunday, Sherman discovered the omission, "stood impulsively" during the service to speak the deleted phrase, and thereafter ordered that the church include Lincoln in its regular prayers or face closure. [10] More serious forms of rebellion, such as spying and smuggling—including among women—occurred with regularity within the occupied city, while guerrilla activity posed the greatest threat in outlying areas. In September 1862, after a guerilla attack on a Union vessel on the river, Sherman ordered the burning of the town of Randolph, about thirty miles north, and he became increasingly pessimistic about the prospects of ever convincing Confederates to return to the Union fold. According to biographers, the experience of confronting die-hard Rebels in Memphis helped shape Sherman's later conception of the need for a harder, more-destructive form of warfare. [11]

While White Memphians resisted Union occupation, African Americans in the surrounding areas viewed the city as an outpost for freedom. In the weeks and months after the battle, just as had occurred around Nashville and New Orleans, enslaved African Americans began fleeing toward federal forces. Thousands of enslaved people from the Delta walked off plantations. President Lincoln's Emancipation Proclamation of January 1, 1863, only accelerated this great migration. While Sherman had established a system for utilizing Black laborers in the city as early as August 1862, the need to accommodate increased numbers of people streaming into the city led to the establishment of "contraband camps" under the authority of the War Department. The name had originated in Union Gen. Benjamin Butler's policy in Virginia of refusing to return fugitive slaves to their Confederate masters, as he deemed the enslaved "contraband" of war—confiscated enemy property. Initially, conditions in these camps were deplorable. Harsh winter weather, inadequate housing, and poor health among those who had arrived in the city led to the deaths of an estimated twelve hundred formerly enslaved people during the winter of 1862-1863. Nevertheless, camps eventually became more self-sustaining, as Northern aid societies provided cloth for freed people to make their own clothing while missionaries and teachers attempted to establish the institutions of church and school. At the peak of their operation in the winter of 1863-1864, contraband camps in Memphis accommodated more than four thousand formerly enslaved people who had entered the city.[12]

For Black men who migrated out of slavery and into freedom, military service offered an opportunity to prove one's manhood as well as one's loyalty to the Union. Approximately seven thousand formerly enslaved men enlisted and trained in the city, and many went on to engage in combat in such places as Brice's Crossroads and Tupelo. Meanwhile, more than 3,000 of these black soldiers were members of the 3rd U.S. Colored Heavy Artillery, which formed in Memphis beginning in June 1863 and garrisoned at Fort Pickering for the rest of the war. Built mostly by Black labor and stretching nearly two miles along the river, the heavily-fortified Fort Pickering served as the city's primary defense.[13]

Throughout the Union occupation, occasional raids by Confederate cavalry in the surrounding region unnerved federal authorities while offering a spark of hope to local residents. One particularly horrific episode stiffened the resolve of White and Black Union soldiers alike. In April 1864, Confederate Gen. Nathan Bedford Forrest attacked the Union garrison at Fort Pillow, just upriver from Memphis, massacring nearly half of the soldiers there, the majority of them African American. When the news made it to Fort Pickering, Black and White officers vowed that "as officers commanding colored troops in the service of the Union, we now know our doom if we are captured by our enemies, but that far from being intimidated thereby, we accept the issue, and adopt as our significant motto 'Victory or death.'"[14] Later that summer, Forrest executed an early morning raid into Memphis, as he attempted to capture Union generals, release Confederate prisoners at the Irving Block Prison on Court Square, and force the recall of Union troops from northern Mississippi. Forrest failed in the first two objectives—one of the Union generals narrowly escaped down an alley in his nightshirt—but the Rebel commander succeeded in cutting telegraph wires, taking prisoners and supplies, and forcing the Union to withdraw some forces from Mississippi in order to defend the city.

The war concluded in spring 1865, resulting in the preservation of the Union and the eventual abolition of slavery, but events during the preceding four years cast a long shadow over Memphis. The experience of occupation and the spirit of defiance that it produced set the tone for White behavior in the years and decades that followed. Just as important was the demographic revolution brought about by those moving out of slavery. Between 1860 and 1865, the city's African American population increased at least four-fold, from fewer than 3,900 to approximately twenty thousand by the war's end.[15]

In the short term, White resentment toward the city's Black newcomers manifested itself in the horror of the Memphis Massacre of 1866. In the months after Confederate surrender, the ongoing presence of Black troops at Fort Pickering continued to offend local Whites, and a confrontation between Black troops and White police officers in May 1866 turned violent. With tensions between Black and White residents, especially the Irish, already simmering, White mobs lashed out in three days of indiscriminate violence against the Black community. When the mayhem had subsided, at least forty-six African Americans had lost their lives and another seventy to eighty had sustained wounds. Other Blacks were robbed and raped, while more than one hundred buildings—homes, businesses, churches, and schools—burned down. Outraged congressional leaders dispatched a three-man committee to investigate. Later that summer, Thaddeus Stevens, a leading Republican member of Congress, invoked "the screams and groans of the dying victims at Memphis" in a speech in support of the landmark Fourteenth Amendment to the Constitution.[16] Ratified two years later, the amendment established citizenship and civil rights for all those born in the United States. In a sense, those who suffered at the hands of racist mobs in Memphis helped make possible the foundation of American civil rights law.

In the decades that followed, as the federal government retreated from its enforcement of Reconstruction-era civil rights, White Memphians reasserted control over the Black population. By the dawn of the twentieth century, legal segregation and extra-legal lynching defined the relationship between White and Black southerners, while the romantic Lost Cause version of the Civil War came to dominate historical memory of the conflict. The Lost Cause exalted the bravery of Southern soldiers in the face of overwhelming odds, while justifying the secessionist cause as rooted in constitutional principle rather than racial oppression. In May 1901, Memphis hosted a three-day Confederate reunion, during which participants laid the cornerstone for the city's first monument, a twenty-one-and-a-half-feet-tall equestrian sculpture of Forrest. Although at the time of his death in 1877 Memphians expressed ambivalent attitudes about the antebellum slave trader, wartime general, and post-war Ku Klux Klan leader and businessman, by the early twentieth century "the Wizard of the Saddle" had emerged as a larger-than-life figure in the city. Known for his daring raids into Union-held territory, the hometown hero came to symbolize the rough-hewn values of the rural Whites who migrated into Memphis after the city's devastating Yellow Fever epidemics.[17] Although originally buried at Elmwood Cemetery, the bodies of Forrest and his wife were moved and re-buried near the center of town in 1905, when local notables unveiled and dedicated the Forrest monument. In accepting the statue on behalf of the city, Mayor J.J. Williams noted confidently that future generations, especially women, "will see to it that this statue will be cared for and prized, while speaking, as it will to the coming ages, of a chivalric race, of a glorious past, and of a glorious Forrest."[18]

By the second half of the twentieth century, the Lost Cause continued to hold Memphis in its grasp. Several admiring biographies, along with a best-selling 1952 novel about the Battle of Shiloh by the young Delta-born writer Shelby Foote, portrayed Forrest as a military genius and as "the most man in the world." With Forrest's mythical status secure in Memphis, in 1955 the Tennessee Historical Commission erected a marker that identified the site of Forrest's "antebellum home" and lauded him for his "business enterprises."[19] Intentionally suppressing the more unsavory aspects of Forrest's life, the marker neglected to mention that his residence on Adams had stood adjacent to his slave mart and that his business was buying and selling people. Nine years later, as Congress enacted the Civil Rights Act of 1964 over the fierce objections of White southerners, Memphians erected a statue to another local hero, Jefferson Davis, who had resided briefly in the city after the war. Noting his service as president of the Confederacy, the inscription simply described him, with no irony, as "a true American patriot." In the face of momentous changes in American civil rights law, many White Memphians remained resistant. In spring 1968, Martin Luther King Jr., one of the twentieth century's greatest human rights leaders, took an assassin's bullet in the neck while in the city to assist striking sanitation workers. Even in the aftermath of this tragic episode, as Whites increasingly fled the city and Blacks gained more political power, the city's Confederate monuments remained.

Through secession and war, Union occupation and Black migration, White violence and Black resistance, the history of the Civil War and its legacy in Memphis is long, complicated, and oppressive. Yet, at the end of the second decade of the twenty-first century, signs of change abound. After a young White supremacist who had embraced Confederate symbols murdered nine African Americans at a Charleston, South Carolina, church in 2015, White Americans began a national re-examination of Confederate monuments, a process that accelerated after a 2017 "Unite the Right" rally in Charlottesville, Virginia, resulted in the death of a counter-protester. Beginning in 2015, a handful of monuments came down across the country. Memphis, too, began to come to terms with its past. In 2016, citizens dedicated the first marker acknowledging the Memphis Massacre of 1866, and local grass-roots activists—led by Take 'em Down 901—held a series of protests calling for the removal of the Confederate statues. In response, on December 20, 2017, Mayor Jim Strickland, the city's first White mayor since 1991, announced that the city had sold to a non-profit agency the two city parks in which the Forrest and Davis statues stood, sidestepping a state law designed to protect such monuments. No longer on city property, the monuments came down that night. A little more than three months later, on the fiftieth anniversary of King's assassination in Memphis, community members dedicated a new marker at the site of the Forrest slave mart—a marker that tells the real story of what happened there.[20]

After more than a century, the pro-white supremacist Lost Cause version of the conflict that has dominated the cultural landscape seems to be losing its grip. Perhaps the next step in our city's long relationship with the Civil War will be to erect monuments to the real heroes—the thousands of African American men, women, and children who risked their lives to leave plantations to come to Memphis in search of freedom.

CHAPTER FIVE

A MASSACRE IN MEMPHIS

Stephen V. Ash

The last 140 miles of Congressman Elihu Washburne's railroad journey from Washington to Memphis spanned the flat countryside of west Tennessee. Cotton plantations dominated the landscape: from the train window Washburne would have seen broad stretches of fenced and tilled land alternating with patches of woods, with here and there a planter's manor and a scattering of laborers' cabins. Black people were at work in the fields with hoes and plows. The fields were green, not white, for the full ripening of the crop was still months away.

It was Tuesday, May 22, three weeks to the day since the outbreak of the horrific race riot in Memphis that had riveted the nation. Washburne, a long-serving Republican member of the House of Representatives from Illinois, had been charged with overseeing Congress's investigation of the riot. This was an important assignment: the bloody, three-day upheaval, the most sensational event outside Washington since the death of the Confederacy, would no doubt play a key role in the crucial decisions now facing the nation.

Washburne already knew a good deal about the riot and its causes. In the months leading up to the riot he had received letters from acquaintances in Memphis concerning the situation there, particularly the city's racial and political tensions. Newspapers had provided considerable information on the riot itself. Moreover, both the local military commandant and the Freedmen's Bureau had already investigated the riot, although not as extensively as Washburne planned to, and he had been informed about their findings.

From these various sources he had learned that there was a bitter, long-standing antipathy between Memphis's blacks and lower-class whites. The Union army had taken the city early in the war, in 1862, paving the way for emancipated slaves from the countryside. This had the effect of greatly aggravating the old bitterness, because the newly arrived blacks began to compete with the lower-class whites for jobs. The city police — who were all white, nearly all Irish immigrants, and notoriously unprofessional

— especially detested the freed people and regularly abused them. The thuggishness of the police went unchecked by the leading civil officials of the city, who were themselves mostly Irish and contemptuous of the blacks. The soldiers of the black U.S. Army regiment that had garrisoned the city until they were mustered out just before the riot were a special target of white resentment: this resentment was not altogether unjustified, however, for the unit was poorly disciplined and some of its men stirred up trouble or committed crimes when off duty. The native-born Southern whites of Memphis had been, with few exceptions, devout secessionists during the war — many hundreds had served in the Confederate army — and they remained unrepentant now, resentful of Union victory and federal authority, furious about their political disenfranchisement, hostile to equal rights for the freed people, and contemptuous of the Yankee newcomers in their city. Almost all the local newspapers were controlled by such Rebels, and in the months leading up to the riot they ran lurid editorials that further inflamed the prejudice against blacks and Northerners.

The riot, which was triggered by clashes between black men and police officers on April 30 and May 1, was an explosion of rage and violence directed against the freed people and perpetrated by the white underclass. Policemen and firemen were among the rioters, as were certain higher-ranking officers of the city government. By the time the rioting ended on May 3, at least forty blacks had been murdered, dozens more wounded, several raped, and many others robbed. Many black churches, schools, and residences had been torched.

Many of these shocking details made it into the reports of newspapers around the country, which rightly saw the riot as a major development in the increasingly rancorous debate over the future of the South, and indeed the whole nation. The Civil War had resolved two momentous, long-standing issues: the attempt of eleven Southern states to gain independence was crushed, and slavery was abolished. But new questions soon arose: How were the seceded states to be restored to the Union? How was the devastated Southern economy to be rebuilt? How were the defeated Rebels to be dealt with? And what about black Southerners, whose freedom was assured but whose status was otherwise undefined? Implicit in these questions were others even more profound and far-reaching: Did this task of postwar reconstruction, as Abraham Lincoln had hinted at Gettysburg, offer the opportunity to forge an essentially new and greater American nation? If so, how could that be achieved?

Congressman Washburne's judgments on the great postwar questions placed him squarely in his party's mainstream. Republicans insisted that the Rebels who had fought so hard to fracture the Union and preserve slavery must truly accept defeat and emancipation, must confess and atone for the sins of secession and rebellion, and must demonstrate by word and deed that they were now loyal U.S. citizens. Until they did, their states must be denied congressional and electoral representation and their own political activity must be circumscribed. Republicans also insisted that the freed slaves must have sufficient legal—and, if necessary, military—protection to give substance to their freedom and to prevent their abuse and exploitation at the hands of the Rebels. Restoring the South to the Union and fully reenfranchising its white citizenry without reforming its flawed society and institutions and ideology would, as the Republicans saw it, invite continued sectional disputes of the kind that had brought on the war, render meaningless the terrible sacrifices the North had made in putting down the Southern rebellion, and prevent the realization of Lincoln's vision for the nation's future.

In the first postwar Congress, which was dominated by Republicans, Washburne was named to the newly created Joint Committee on Reconstruction. In early 1866 the committee held hearings on conditions in the South and generated evidence that put the Republicans more and more at odds with President Andrew Johnson. Johnson, a Southern Unionist and Democrat, wanted the former Confederate states to be speedily restored to the Union with no fundamental changes besides the abolition of slavery. He also wanted the Rebels to be reenfranchised with minimal qualifications, and he was content to let them deal with the freed people pretty much as they saw fit. In the immediate postwar months he liberally granted amnesty and pardons to former Confederates and allowed them to take part in elections and constitutional conventions that set up new state governments. (Those in Tennessee, however, were subject to somewhat different terms and remained disenfranchised.) Democrats in Congress and across the nation cheered Johnson's policy. The president's vetoes, in February and March 1866, of two bills intended to protect the emancipated slaves outraged the Republicans, who then began formulating a constitutional amendment that would make their demands into law.

The unthinkable carnage of the Memphis riot thus occurred at a particularly charged moment. It threw the debates in Washington into stark relief—it made what was at stake in them unavoidably clear and, because many policemen had not just condoned but had taken part in the massacre, called into question the very foundation on which every classically liberal government rests its legitimacy: its guarantee to protect its citizens from being murdered. Something had to be done; to some congressmen, it may have seemed that the nation's future, which had supposedly been decided by the war, was again hanging in the balance. Eleven days after the riot finally ended, the House of Representatives passed a resolution creating the Select Committee on the Memphis Riots.

Washburne, its chairman, arrived in the city with his fellow committee members on the twenty-second, at the Memphis and Ohio Railroad depot on the city's north side. From there it was a one-mile hack ride south along Main Street to the Gayoso House, the city's finest hotel, where a room had been reserved for the committee's hearings. Little or no evidence of the riot's violence and destruction was visible along this route, so Washburne and his colleagues did not immediately see the charred, collapsed remains of houses, shanties, schools, and churches and, in some of the cemeteries, the dozens of freshly filled graves.

At this time of year, if the weather was sunny and dry as it was on this day, one of the first things a visitor such as Washburne could not have helped noticing was the dust. It rose in clouds from the streets and billowed outward, stirred up by the ceaseless traffic of buggies, hacks, carts, drays, and wagons, some driven at breakneck speed, in violation of the law. For years the city authorities had considered paving the major thoroughfares but so far had done nothing more than talk about it. Business owners on a few of the primary commercial streets, including Main, pooled money to hire a man to ply their streets in a cart equipped with a barrel of water and a sprinkler. This helped, but dust in lesser quantities wafted in from unsprinkled streets nearby. Everywhere in the city, dust settled on clothing, drifted down onto porches and sidewalks, and crept indoors through open windows. Housewives, maids, and shopkeepers battled it with brooms and feather dusters as they prayed for rain. But when rain came it turned the streets into a muddy quagmire, six inches deep or more, and the people prayed for clear skies.

Another thing that immediately struck the visitor to Memphis was the crowding. The city proper stretched for more than two miles along the east bank of the Mississippi River and more than a mile inland, but even with the adjacent unincorporated neighborhoods commonly regarded as part of the city, there was scant room for the thirty-five or forty thousand people who now lived there — or were thought to, for the number of inhabitants was uncertain. All anybody knew for sure was that the population had swelled since the census takers of 1860 had counted twenty-three thousand Memphians. Newcomers, whites in addition to newly freed blacks, had inundated the city after its capture by Union forces in June 1862, and the end of the war and of military rule in 1865 had not stemmed the tide. The streets teemed with people and the horses, mules, and oxen that served them; in many residences two families crammed into a space meant for one.

On the day of his arrival, Washburne assembled the committee and opened the proceedings in parlor 398 of the Gayoso House, formally confirming the committee's credentials for the record. The real work began at ten o'clock the next morning. The first witness was a prominent U.S. Army officer, Major General George Stoneman, commander of the Department of the Tennessee, with headquarters in Memphis. During his lengthy testimony, Stoneman answered questions about his dealings with municipal officials during and after the riot, the threats made during the riot against the city's Northern-born population, the makeup of the riotous mobs, and the sentiments of the Memphis newspapers. He contradicted reports in the Rebel papers that blacks had actually perpetrated the violence. It "was no negro riot," he said firmly. "The negroes had nothing to do with the riot, except to be killed and abused."

The next day, the committee questioned several Memphis residents who had witnessed the rioting. One was Ellen Dilts, a homemaker and Yankee immigrant. She told of hearing a policeman exclaim to a crowd of whites, "Kill every nigger, no matter who, men or women." Also questioned was a shoemaker and former slave named Albert Harris, who was not just an eyewitness to the riot but one of its victims. On the night of May 2 a gang of white men, some of them policemen, had forced their way into his house, held a pistol to his head in front of his frantic, sobbing wife, robbed him, and threatened to burn his place down.

That day, the twenty-fourth, Washburne wrote a letter to one of his Republican colleagues on the Joint Committee. The Select Committee had begun work, he reported, "and it is plain to see we have a long job before us." There were many more witnesses he intended to call and, although he had already reached some general conclusions, there was much more he wanted to know about the origin and course of the riot, about its perpetrators and victims, and about this dusty, crowded, deeply divided city. Fueling this quest was Washburne's fervent engagement with the great postwar questions, and his intuition that the riot held the answers to many of them. "I intend to remain here," he vowed, "till we get to the bottom of this business."

***

The 1866 Memphis riot was one of the earliest—and would remain one of the bloodiest—battles in a vast counterrevolution carried out by white men in the South who were determined to deny full freedom and equality to the former slaves among them. This counterrevolution provoked the U.S. government to take extraordinary measures to protect the freed people, measures that launched one of the most remarkable periods in the South's history, which historians call the era of Radical reconstruction. Ironically, however, the Memphis riot, having assisted at the birth of Radical reconstruction, also had a hand in its death.

In the congressional elections of 1866, Northern Republican candidates and the Republican press invoked the riot (along with other incidents of white violence in the South since the war ended) to condemn President Johnson's policies of letting the ex-Confederates restore their state governments on their own and deal with the freed people as they saw fit. This line of attack worked: in the elections, the party substantially reinforced its majorities in the House and Senate.

In early March 1867 Congress passed, over the president's veto, an act with which it seized control of reconstruction and struck down Johnson's program. This act and its subsequent amendments abolished (with one exception) the resurrected Southern state governments recognized by Johnson, imposed temporary federal military rule on those ten states, and decreed a strict procedure they would have to follow to restore their governments and be readmitted to the Union. The key provisos were that they must adopt new state constitutions that granted black men the right to vote and must ratify the Fourteenth Amendment. The Memphis riot again figured prominently in the deliberations that produced this legislation; the act's preamble asserted that in the former Rebel states there was no "adequate protection for life or property."

All ten states were readmitted within three years, and in the ensuing period of Radical reconstruction — which varied in duration from state to state, but was wholly ended by 1877 — Republican-dominated state governments, elected by the votes of freedmen and white "scalawags" and "carpetbaggers," pursued a vision of biracial democracy, legal equality for the freed people, public education for the children of both races, and economic development (while not infrequently engaging in fraud and graft).

But the interpretation of the Memphis riot endorsed by the authors and proponents of the congressional reconstruction act, based mostly on the federal investigations, was not the only one that influenced public opinion. The Conservative interpretation of the riot depicted it as an understandable, if excessive, reaction to the insufferable provocations of the freed slaves—who were unrestrained by law or morality and whipped into a frenzy by meddling Yankees—and extolled its salutary lessons for blacks. Here, in other words, was further evidence that emancipation had been a grievous mistake, that the freed people were dangerously out of control, and that violence in the service of white supremacy was justified and indeed necessary. These beliefs fueled the clandestine, guerrilla-style terrorism of organizations such as the Ku Klux Klan and later the paramilitary onslaughts of the White League, the Red Shirts, and the like, which challenged the Republican state regimes in the South.

Pressured by Northerners who had grown disgusted with the seeming inability of the freedmen and their scalawag and carpetbagger friends to maintain order in the Southern states and govern them honestly, the federal government eventually stopped intervening to protect the Republican governments, standing aside as the last of them fell. The Rebel "redeemers" promptly undid nearly all the progressive accomplishments of the Republican regimes (while generally perpetuating the fraud and graft) and gradually relegated blacks to the bottom tier of a new racial caste system that endured into the second half of the twentieth century. Thus did the Memphis riot, having helped usher in the extraordinary experiment of Radical reconstruction, also help obliterate it and pave the way for its successor, the New South era of black disenfranchisement and Jim Crow segregation.

There is another irony in all of this. The Memphis riot, which played so prominent a role in persuading Northerners to reject Johnsonian reconstruction and embrace Congress's alternative, occurred in the only former Rebel state not at the time dominated politically by ex-Confederates. Tennessee was in fact exempted from the congressional reconstruction act because it was under Republican control and had (in July 1866) ratified the Fourteenth Amendment, had immediately thereafter been readmitted to the Union by congressional resolution, and had (in February 1867) enfranchised its black male inhabitants (thereby becoming the first Southern state to do so). Moreover, the main perpetrators of the Memphis riot were not ex-Confederates, but Irish immigrants who had not served the Rebel cause. The Northerners who waved the bloody shirt of the Memphis riot did not always mention these facts. Those who did often insisted that the city's Rebel press had incited the Irish to riot.

The riot in fact resists any easy characterization, Republican, Conservative, or otherwise. As much as it told contemporaries about the state of their nation, and as much as it tells us today about the Civil War era and the origins of the Jim Crow South, the riot was a highly distinctive event, and Memphis in 1866 was a highly distinctive city. Paradoxically, the extraordinary sources that the riot left in its wake are the kind of thing historians who study the nineteenth century long for, yet they simultaneously vex the historian, whose job it is to analyze, synthesize, and contextualize, to make order out of chaos. Another way of putting this is to say that the Memphis riot raises challenging questions about the history historians write. Perhaps this is why the riot has not been extensively written about before now.

For instance, while the riot was very much a part of the broad phenomenon of white reactionary violence in the reconstruction South, it differed in significant ways from the other instances of that violence. It was a spontaneous, unorganized event in a city, which set it apart from the planned, well-organized, and predominantly rural mayhem of the Klan, the White League, and similar groups. It differed from that mayhem, too, in that its perpetrators were, for the most part, not ex-Confederates. This same fact set the riot in Memphis apart from those in New Orleans and other Southern cities during reconstruction.

Moreover, the Southern white counterrevolution of the reconstruction era is not the only historical context within which the Memphis riot can be meaningfully situated. It can also be seen as a late manifestation of the mobbing of blacks by whites during the insurrection panics that intermittently seized the antebellum South and reared up again in December 1865. It can be seen, too, as an instance of the periodic mob violence inflicted on blacks by working-class whites in urban America (mostly in the North) in the mid-nineteenth century—notably the horrific New York City riot of 1863. Nor would it be unreasonable to cite the riot as an early instance of the racial lynching that appeared in the postemancipation South and rose to a gruesome intensity in the early years of the twentieth century. In this sense, the Memphis riot illustrates the power of racism and mob psychology to turn ordinary human beings into vicious, conscienceless killers. All of these interpretations are useful and valid, but when the riot is placed too confidently in any one of them, it begins to stick out.

The origin and nature of the riot further set it apart from ostensibly similar events. For one thing, it bears repeating that the rioters were almost all Irish-American. This fact was attested to by witness after witness in the official investigations—blacks, Southern whites, and Yankees alike (few Irish were questioned). This testimony is persuasive for two reasons besides its sheer volume. First, the great majority of Irish immigrants in that era were readily distinguishable by their manners and accents and in many cases by their dress. Second, while the Southern white witnesses might have had reason to exaggerate the guilt of the Irish, in order to absolve their own class, the blacks had much less reason and the Yankees none: if native-born white Southerners (who were also readily distinguishable to contemporary observers) had made up a significant portion of the riotous mobs, the freed people and Yankees would certainly have said so.

Yet here the historian runs into another obstacle: the Irish rioters were a very small segment of Memphis's Irish male population. Exactly how small it is impossible to say, for the number of rioters can only be guessed at. The mobs described by reliable witnesses seem to have numbered in no case more than a few dozen men, but of course there were many different mobs at work in various parts of the city over the three days of rioting. Considering that some individuals accompanied more than one mob, a very generous estimate of the total number of rioters would be two or three hundred—including policemen and citizens who professed to be acting officially. This is a small portion indeed of the Irish male inhabitants of the city and suburbs, who (children included) probably numbered at least three thousand. Simply blaming the Irish for the riot is thus unfair, and can seem to involve the person doing the blaming in a racial calculus similar to that of the city's elite Rebels of the time.

Though the actions of the rioters are unpardonable, the Irish in Memphis had, as they saw it, good reasons for disliking blacks. They too struggled to survive and be accepted in America, and saw blacks as rivals in that twofold quest. The revolutionary events between mid-1862 and early 1866 saw enslaved Memphians emancipated and thousands of other newly free blacks flock to the city to escape the plantations. These freed people crowded into neighborhoods throughout the city, established communal institutions, competed with the Irish for jobs, took up arms as Union soldiers, and sometimes got drunk and rowdy and committed crimes. Having thus gained and asserted freedom, they insisted that that freedom must be more than nominal, and they were aided and defended by Northerners.

Irish resentment of blacks, in other words, had more proximate causes than the national political situation, which may explain why the role of the city's Rebel press in provoking the Irish to violence was overstated by Republicans. The newspapers were certainly racist (and anti-Yankee), fiercely so in some cases, and they often denounced the character and behavior of the freed people so viciously as to utterly dehumanize them. They also repeatedly declared that the city would be better off without the blacks, or at least most of them. But whether the Irish paid much attention to any of this is questionable. As the voice of the Rebel elite, the papers were generally condescending and often downright disparaging toward the Irish and could not have appealed much to those Irish who were inclined (and able) to read. And, in any event, the Irish needed no prodding by others to be roused to destructive fury against the freed people. Even had there been no Rebel press in Memphis in 1865-66, there would very likely still have been a riot.

It was the city's Southern-born whites, much more than the Irish, who took the rhetoric of the Rebel press to heart. But then what is the historian supposed to make of the fact that they did not join the Irish rioters, at least not in significant numbers? There are a few possible answers. In many cases paternalist ties bound white Southerners and former slaves; such ties were almost wholly absent in black-Irish relations. But the Rebels were certainly capable of murderous assaults on the freed people. This was made clear beginning in 1868, when west Tennessee became the scene of extensive Ku Klux Klan violence. That violence seems, however, to have been provoked mostly by the political activism of the recently enfranchised freedmen. It may be that in 1866, with the ex-slaves still unenfranchised, west Tennessee Rebels did not yet feel sufficiently aggrieved to wreak bloody, large-scale vengeance on blacks. Or it may be that once the Memphis riot was under way, the city's Rebels, deeming it an Irish affair and generally contemptuous of the Irish, chose to stay out of it.

Yet to say that Rebels played little role in the riot, and that Rebel newspapers were not to blame for inciting it, is not to say that Republicans were altogether mistaken or deceitful in using the riot as evidence for their cause. Numerous witnesses swore to hearing rioters damn emancipation, damn the Yankees who aided and protected the freed people, and declare their intention to kill or burn out as many blacks as they could and scare the rest out of the city, along with their Yankee friends. That these expressions of the rioters' sentiments and aims were uttered by presumably loyal Irish immigrants rather than unrepentant Rebels may have diminished their relevance to the argument for the congressional reconstruction act; but they were nevertheless good evidence for the broader argument that Southern blacks' freedom and rights and indeed lives were threatened and that they, along with the Northerners who stood by them, needed federal protection. (The Conservative claim that the riot demonstrated the need to reenfranchise Tennessee's "respectable" whites, so they could regain control of the city from the Irish and thus protect the ex-slaves, is unpersuasive. A Rebel-controlled city government would not likely have proved a better steward of the freed people's safety and interests than the Irish-controlled government. The New Orleans municipal government, it should be noted, was under Rebel control at the time of the riot in that city.)

Further complicating things is the fact that, while Irishmen were the main perpetrators of the riot, the incident that ignited it — the clash between the four Irish policemen and the raucous crowd of black ex-soldiers on South Street on the afternoon of May 1 — cannot be blamed on the Irish. The policemen did exceed their authority in trying to disperse the revelers, who were congregated just outside the city limit; the policemen knew this, but nevertheless obeyed Recorder Creighton's command. The black men were within their rights to ignore the order to disperse. However, when the policemen, recognizing the futility of their mission, broke off the encounter and retreated up the street toward the bayou bridge, the matter should have ended there. The blacks were wrong to follow and harass them, and wrong to fire their pistols into the air. The policemen cannot be blamed for assuming they were being shot at and returning fire. It goes without saying that the misconduct of the ex-soldiers in this incident in no way justified the savage mob assaults on South Memphis that ensued, but the tidy story about blacks' victimization at the hands of whites does not entirely hold up.

One of the few aspects of the riot that can be known with precision is the number of whites who died in it, for the Rebel press gave it much attention. (The Select Committee's total of forty-six blacks killed, while probably not exactly correct for various reasons, is likely near the mark.) To the Select Committee's total of two whites — policeman John Stevens, who died of the wound accidentally self-inflicted in the initial shootout at the bayou bridge, and fireman Henry Dunn, shot a short while later by John Pendergrast, who mistook him for a black — should be added a third: Benjamin Dennis, gunned down in a saloon on May 2 by a fireman for talking with a freedman. That none of these three white victims died at the hands of a black person is worth reiterating.

CHAPTER SIX

A CITY OF CORPSES:
YELLOW FEVER IN MEMPHIS

Molly Caldwell Crosby

"I suspect that the Memphis sorrow (yellow fever epidemic)
is greatly exaggerated by the panic-stricken people."
— President Rutherford B. Hayes, *August 1878*[1]

"It is impossible to estimate with any approach to accuracy,
the loss to the country occasioned by this epidemic."
— President Rutherford B. Hayes, *December 1878*[2]

No historian or writer can really convey the devastation and horror
of the 1878 yellow fever epidemic. J.M. Keating tried. He was the managing
editor of the Memphis *Appeal*, later to become *The Commercial Appeal*. At one
point, he alone was left in the offices, reporting what he saw each day and
printing pages himself. Of the epidemic, he wrote, "An appalling gloom
hung over the doomed city...There were hours, especially at night, when
the solemn oppressions of universal death bore upon the human mind...
Not a sound was to be heard; the silence was painfully profound. Death
prevailed everywhere. Trade and traffic were suspended. The energies of
all who remained were enlisted in the struggle with death."[3]

Today, when Memphis makes news, it's not always for positive
reasons. We own a mixed and complicated history. But, 140 years ago, with
a singular focus, the world waited for news from Memphis. Thousands of
people lined up in cities like Boston, New York, and Philadelphia, offering
their help. As Keating himself said, "The cry for food, for clothing, for
money, for doctors, for as many as a thousand coffins, went out by telegraph
to the ends of the earth, and a prompt and generous response came back...
The contagion of kindness passed beyond the limits of our own country"
to France, England, Germany, India, Australia, South America.[4]

The Memphis of the 1870s held a promising future. It was one of the
largest cities in the South, twice the size of Atlanta.[5] It had been chosen as

a bluff city on the precipice of the American South and an immense, new frontier. The only thing separating the two was the treacherous Mississippi River, a huge gash in the American landscape. Murky, ochre-colored and unpredictable, the river pushed against levees, dividing the town from the dense forests and willow thickets of Arkansas. It was the last stop before heading west, and it was the point of entry back into the world of the Old South. But it wasn't just the topography that gave Memphis a startling sense of contrast; it was the people. All classes of society, all colors of skin, all manner of accents migrated to a fault line carved between the past and the future, the Old South and the new frontier.

As the latticework of American transportation and expansion spread westward, Memphis remained at a crossroads; steamboats ran north to south, and railroads connected it to the East Coast. Surrounded by rural states and plantations, Memphis became a hub: the largest inland cotton market.[6] As the Bluff City sloped toward the river, levees piled high with crates of tufted white, Memphis looked like a town built upon cotton. But the city's place at the center of so much expansion is what would also mark its tragic place in history.

The story began with a voyage. A shipment of sugar set sail from Havana on board the screw steamer the *Emily B. Souder* in the spring of that year. As the *Souder* approached the New Orleans port authority, she dropped anchor and awaited the quarantine officer. The captain knew he had two feverish crewmen, but if the *Souder* failed inspection, she would be quarantined, forced to raise the "yellow jack" flag, and delay the shipment for two weeks. The captain made the fateful decision to lie, hiding the sick crewmen to pass inspection. He sailed freely into New Orleans, where the crewmen grew worse and died within days.[7]

The physician in the dead house examined one of the bodies, describing it in his notes as "bright canary color."[8] While fevers and illness are common among ship trade in the Caribbean, there is no other disease that leaves such dramatic coloring. Yellow fever, he realized, had arrived in New Orleans.

The inspecting physician had just received a telegram that week from the Tennessee Board of Health inquiring about fevers in the port town. The physician returned a telegram, making no mention of the fever nor the dead crewmembers.[9] Ship trade continued; commerce prevailed. Other ships bobbed alongside the *Souder*, loading cargo and charting courses up the Mississippi River.

As the vessels approached Memphis, the view was impressive. White marble buildings, many designed by the same architect who designed the Mall in Washington, DC, lined the bluffs. The Italian-styled customs house, still under construction, towered over cobblestone levees. As the sun sank over Arkansas, the light crawled across the dark, thrashing river and coppered the buildings of the Memphis skyline.

Insects pricked the dusk, flying low across the river's surface. A warm spring arrived unusually early that year. Plants bloomed before their time. Humidity edged ahead of summer.[10] Although no one at the time knew what had brought the premature heat, scientists later identified it as an El Niño cycle. Most yellow fever epidemics, in fact, would be linked to El Niño weather patterns when there is a spike in vectors and vector-born disease alike.[11]

As boats docked for the evening, passengers made their way past the shanty-towns at the river's edge toward the Pinch District. The neighborhood was a poor one, crowded with river traffic, drunken laughter, the roll of bone dice, the smell of fish in iron skillets, and worse. In spite of the city's prosperity, Memphis had more than its fair share of filth and poverty. Like most major cities, progress outpaced the ability to accommodate it. The Gayoso Bayou, running in a series of stagnant pools through the Pinch, frothed with raw sewage, garbage, even dead farm animals. It was hardly surprising then that it was here, in the Pinch, that the first case of yellow fever was reported. In reality, several cases had already slipped silently into city streets.[12]

When the *Appeal* published the first case of fever, officials warned against panic, but it was of little use. Memphians had experienced yellow fever epidemics before with small eruptions in the 1850s and 1860s, followed by the larger epidemic of 1873. The fear of the fever traveled far beyond the city as well. As "YELLOW FEVER IN MEMPHIS" flashed across telegraph wires nationwide, the news chilled residents from New York to Philadelphia to Charleston and every town, small or large, that fed from the Mississippi River.[13]

While epidemic disease was nothing new to American cities, and cholera, typhoid, smallpox, among others, had taken many more lives, yellow fever educed a unique fear among Americans. In part, that was due to fear of the unknown. It wasn't until 1900 that Walter Reed would prove the virus was spread by mosquitoes. But it also arose from the horrors of the virus itself.[14] A hemorrhagic fever, the virus attacks organs and blood vessels alike. Patients bleed through their mouths, eyes, nose, and ears. Internal bleeding and digested blood cause the tell-tale "black vomit." Fever, sometimes as high as 105 degrees, causes delirium. As with other organs, the liver fails, releasing bile and giving the fever its euphemistic name.

The dread of this disease also stemmed from its long history in the Americas. The virus made its way to this country through the African slave trade, and it devastated port towns. Even today, in New York City, there are twenty thousand yellow fever and cholera victims buried beneath Washington Square Park.[15] Philadelphia, which housed the U.S. capital in the 1790s, saw a yellow fever epidemic so disastrous, it shut down the federal government. George Washington, Thomas Jefferson and John Adams escaped the city; Alexander Hamilton contracted the fever but survived.[16] By the end of the 1793 epidemic, Philadelphia had lost one-tenth of its population, and the U.S. capital moved to Washington, DC.[17] Likewise, the southern ports of Charleston and New Orleans had experienced their own crushing epidemics. Close ties to the slave trade, and its grim march through port cities, led to yellow fever, above all other diseases, becoming known as the *American Plague*.[18]

As news of the 1878 epidemic spread, Memphians fled their city in droves, sometimes leaving doors to their homes wide open and tables still set with silver, filling boats, wagons, and train cars to capacity only to be met by shotgun quarantines along roads and bridges leading into other towns. Refugee camps sprang up throughout the region. In the North, pine was cut to begin building coffins.

Half of the population – roughly twenty-five thousand Memphians – fled in less than a week. Stores and apothecaries closed, food carts emptied, milkmen ceased their rounds, banks shuttered. The trains rolled away; boats bypassed the docks. As Memphis was quarantined from the rest of the world, a morbid calmness fell over the city, so still and quiet as to be serene if one didn't know it was simply the pallor of death. By September of that year, only nineteen thousand people remained in Memphis and seventeen thousand of them contracted yellow fever.[19]

One national news correspondent brave enough to visit the city wrote, "A stranger in Memphis might believe he was in hell." Black smoke twined in the air above fever fires burning the belongings of the dead. Lime and carbolic acid coated the surface of landscapes like fresh snowfall.

The suffocating silence was broken only by church bells tolling burials and wagons slowly rolling through the streets calling, "Bring out your dead!"[20] Soon, the sick and the dying overwhelmed the healthy. Coffins lined sidewalks. Bodies were located by low-flying carrions circling and pecking. Some were so badly decomposed, workers needed shovels. One mother, the paper reported, was found with her infant still in her arms where she died trying to breastfeed. The two were buried together. Death, it was said, could be smelled for miles outside of the city.[21]

When a disaster strikes, the people who stay behind to help are often at risk. In a fire, earthquake or hurricane, with physical devastation all around, first responders consider the risk worth the chance to save lives. In an epidemic, there is no physical damage. No burned buildings or fallen trees. No flooded streets. A place remains eerily unchanged and yet totally devastated. Those who traveled to Memphis or stayed behind faced almost certain death. What's more, just over a decade after the Civil War, the federal government had no organized system of emergency relief. That left the overwhelming management of the epidemic to ordinary doctors, nurses, priests, and nuns who have become known as the Martyrs of Memphis. Many left their stories behind in diaries or letters that came to an abrupt stop sometime in September of that year. Two of the most well-known are Reverend Charles Parsons and Sister Constance.

Charles Parsons was a lean man with a soldier's build. He had carved cheekbones, fair hair, a handlebar moustache, and a tender smile. Not a single surviving letter describes him as anything other than gentle and great; and in spite of being a Yankee, Charles Parsons was one of the most beloved rectors in Memphis.

During the Civil War, Parsons had been a northern officer and a hero. At the Battle of Perryville in Kentucky, he continued operating a gun single-handedly, after all of the men in his company had fallen. When the Confederate artillery approached, Charles Parsons held his sword at parade rest and awaited fire. The Confederate colonel, impressed by his courage, ordered his men to hold their fire and allowed Parsons to walk off the battlefield. "That man," the colonel exclaimed, "is too brave to be killed."[22]

After the war, Parsons was encouraged to remain in the military but felt a different calling. He took orders as an Episcopal priest and eventually moved south. Parsons came to Memphis to start anew as rector for Grace Church, where this Union officer now preached to a congregation that included Jefferson Davis and his family. In 1878, only six months before the outbreak of the epidemic, Parsons preached to his congregation about the character of men: "There will come to each of you a time, I trust far away, when the scourge of affliction may fall heavily upon you...wealth, or power, or skill, or even fond affection in the utmost stretch of tenderness, can supply no companion to the soul in its journey through the valley of death."[23] He spoke with the confidence of a soldier who had survived the Civil War, the death of a wife, and the loss of a son to scarlet fever; for all intents and purposes, he had been to that valley of death and returned. Parsons did not know at that moment what lay ahead, that the greatest urban disaster to date awaited them, that when the fever would finally take him, he would have to read his own last rites.

Sister Constance served as sister superior at St. Mary's and was described as "a woman of exquisite grace, tenderness, and loveliness of character, very highly educated, and one who might have adorned the most brilliant social circle."[24] She looked young for her thirty-two years with a round face and blue eyes beneath the heavy black habit, an iron cross around her neck. Constance and the sisters of her order returned from vacation on the Hudson when they heard news of the fever; the sisters were the only ones traveling into Memphis. As the death toll climbed higher each day, it often took the lives of the elderly and adults first. The sisters of St. Mary's turned their cathedral into a ward for the children fast becoming orphaned by this epidemic.

Constance must have set out on her first day with a sense of purpose and strength. Stepping into the heat and stench of Poplar Street, it would not take long to realize the overpowering magnitude of this scourge. The sun, dust, and black smoke coiled around her in a dizzying haze. Victims fell dead in parks, under fences, or alone in their homes, only to be discovered when the heat picked up the scent. There were too many to count.

A man met Constance in the street with a telegram. It was surprising to receive such an official note: *Father and mother are lying dead in the house, brother is dying, send me some help, no money,* signed *Sallie U.*[25]

A number of responders later wrote of the fear that accompanied them the first time they entered a stricken home. They had nursed hundreds from the halls of sick wards, but it was something else entirely to climb the steps of an infected home and enter. The first thing to strike was the smell. It floated into the streets, a scent like rotting hay. The smell grew stronger once inside, where it mingled with soiled sheets, sweat, and vomit. One never knew what to expect—moans, cries, screams, or worse, no sound at all. There was darkness, as windows were boarded shut, and the stagnant heat of imprisoned air hit. Then, as their eyes focused, they saw the bodies. At first it was hard to tell which ones were living and which were not. If deceased, one could never know how long they had been that way.

A pretty young girl in mourning led Constance into the house. Dust floated, effulgent, in the shafts of afternoon light, and the air was heavy as steam. One corpse lay on the sofa, another one on the bed, their skin yellow and tongues black. A tall young man, nearly naked, was also in the bed, delirious, rocking back and forth. His eyes sank deep into his cheekbones ringed by bruised half-moons. Constance called for a doctor and for an undertaker, though she knew it might take days for them to arrive. She sent the child to the make-shift orphanage in her parish. Constance left the small house sick from the stench. As she went in search of more nurses and wagons, she noticed a spectacular sun, a blood orange setting over the Mississippi. How strange, she thought, that one could still find anything beautiful at all.[26]

Only days later, at the orphanage, a ward visitor tapped Constance on the arm to ask her a question and felt the scorched skin. Constance worked as many hours as she could knowing that once the fever took her, many more would die without her help. When she finally collapsed, she would not let the other nuns give her the best mattress, because it would have to be burned after her death.[27] She died on a rainy September morning. As the nuns fell, one by one, they were buried at Elmwood Cemetery, where they remain today laid out in the shape of a cross. By the time of Constance's death, there were two hundred new cases of yellow fever every day in Memphis.[28]

Other stories from every church or synagogue in Memphis followed suit. Louis Schuyler, a young priest from New Jersey, traveled to the city to help the parish after the loss of so many priests and nuns. He fell ill within days, his body carried into the death alley while he was still alive so that his screams would not disturb other patients. A kind nurse went with him, kneeling beside his cot and promising not to leave his side until he passed.[29] One feverish doctor, William Armstrong, had to be held down to keep from rising from his bed to treat more patients.[30] A local prostitute named Annie Cook turned her brothel into a hospital and nursed people—even as they hurled insults at her—until she too died of the fever.[31]

All of the martyrs are buried at Elmwood, their stories living on in the rain-pocked graves, stone angels, and most poignantly of all, the grassy field where more than fourteen hundred people are buried in a mass grave known as *No Man's Land*.

***

The 1878 epidemic stretched the whole of the Mississippi Valley, killing thousands, crippling commerce, and humbling the federal government. The city hardest hit, however, was Memphis with 5,150 lives lost.[32] That is more lives lost than in any U.S. hurricane in over a century.[33] More lives lost than in the attack on Pearl Harbor.[34] More lives lost than on 9/11.[35] In addition to that, thousands of Memphians were displaced or moved away. There were calls simply to raze the city to the ground. Memphis voted away its charter and did not regain it for another fourteen years.[36]

It also proved to be the last great yellow fever outbreak on American soil, ending over two hundred years of the disease's tenure in the United States. There were a number of reasons for that, some more mysterious than others.

The outlawing of the African slave trade in this hemisphere helped block, in part, the most direct routes from the "yellow fever belt" of Africa.[37] Also, in the wake of this epidemic, the creation of the National Board of Health, a precursor to the Federal Emergency Management Association (FEMA), served as the first federal program to study epidemic diseases and aid quarantined cities.[38]

Quarantine laws also changed. Federal officials as opposed to local ones would now be in charge.[39] Remarkably, the ship responsible for the greatest yellow fever outbreak in U.S. history, the *Emily B. Souder*, sank in December of 1878 as the epidemic finally came to an end.[40]

In Memphis, the most important change was the introduction of sewer systems.[41] Science was correct in implicating water sources, but the reasoning had missed the mark. It was not filthy water contributing to epidemics of yellow fever, but the standing water in cisterns, puddles, and the bayou, that gave mosquitoes breeding grounds.

In addition to that, immigration slowed. Most immigrants from the North, as well as Ireland, Germany, and Eastern Europe, had never before encountered tropical fevers and had little or no immunity. They served almost as kindling to a fever fire.

And, finally, medical advances with the work of Dr. Walter Reed at the turn of the century paved the way for the development of a vaccine—the one still in use today.[42]

The story of yellow fever in Memphis is one of devastation and loss that cast far-reaching shadows over our city, stunting growth for two decades, destroying much of the city's cultural diversity, altering demographics, seeding poverty and racism. Yet the epidemic also shaped much of what we love about Memphis. With it came a steadfast determination to survive, strength, grit, commitment, charity and, above all, hope. That is the true legacy of the epidemic—not tragedy, but triumph, over a plague that likely would have felled any city other than ours.

CHAPTER SEVEN

CREATIVITY AND EXPLOITATION: A HISTORY OF THE MEMPHIS ECONOMY

G. Wayne Dowdy

For two hundred years the economy of Memphis has been characterized by two distinctive factors — exploitation of slave labor and unskilled workers engaged in gritty, low-wage jobs and creativity shown by skilled workers and professionals who built the city's industrial, medical, and distribution infrastructures, developed innovative products and services, and established a vibrant cultural scene. These two elements operated side by side, occasionally overlapping, and sometimes taking advantage of the other in establishing the modern Memphis of the twenty-first century.

When Memphis was laid out in 1819, its population consisted of 251 White residents and 113 African slaves. The city's only business activity was made up of flatboat men transporting commodities through Memphis and small businesses providing goods and services to river workers. Slaves toiled in all of these enterprises, and as the economy grew so did the demand for more labor. In 1830 the slave population of Shelby County had risen to 2,111 and a decade later there were 7,116 slaves in the Memphis area. In addition to struggling in the fields of nearby farms, slaves worked in blacksmith shops and sawmills, drove wagons, built carriages, constructed buildings and maintained the levee. Meanwhile, increased demand for cotton by Northern and European textile mills made Memphis an important transportation hub for the shipment of cotton to market.[1]

Three hundred bales of cotton passed through Memphis in 1825 but within a decade that number had increased to twenty-five thousand. By the mid-1850s, three hundred thousand bales of cotton were shipped through the city. With this increase in the amount of cotton moving through the Bluff City, Memphis declared itself the world's greatest inland cotton market - where speculators bought and sold white gold at the cotton exchange, located at 65 Union Avenue, and farmers shipped the commodity from Memphis to American and European markets. Owing to this commercial traffic, Memphis was the fastest-growing city in the United States in the 1850s. Slaves not only did most of the back-breaking work, they were also a valuable product. Trained carpenters commanded up to $2,500 while field hands were available for $1,000 and a twelve-year-old girl cost $600. The firm owned by Nathan Bedford Forrest, located at 87 Adams, contained facilities for three hundred African slaves that was touted for its "exact and systematic cleanliness, neatness and comfort being strictly observed and enforced...."[2]

The owning of slaves was more than a valuable property for southern whites - they were a symbol of upward mobility and social acceptance. The firm of Bolton, Dickins & Co. took advantage of this sentiment when it stated in an 1855 advertisement that they were "receiving daily large supplies of fresh negroes [sic] from the buying markets....So call and make your purchases to gather your crop - and then call quick again and buy to make another crop. By those means if you will keep up your purchases for ten years there is no telling how much you may be worth. This is the true road to wealth...."[3] The institution of slavery not only denied liberty to millions of Americans it also sparked a sectional conflict that erupted into civil war in April 1861.

Fourteen months later, Memphis was occupied by Union forces which had a profound effect on the local economy. Most local businesses remained loyal to the Confederacy and refused to open, so military commanders allowed goods to pass freely through the city and recruited merchants from Cincinnati and Louisville to open stores in Memphis. Economic activity soon blossomed as did smuggling which funneled twenty million dollars' worth of supplies to the rebel government during the course of the war. Because Memphis fell in June 1862, it was not included in President Abraham Lincoln's Emancipation Proclamation and consequently slavery continued to operate in Memphis until December 1865 when the institution was abolished by the ratification of the Thirteenth Amendment.[4]

After the Civil War cotton continued to drive the city's economy. Unskilled workers ginned and pressed cotton bales, stored them in warehouses and loaded them onto barges and railroad cars while skilled workers graded the cotton and speculators bought and sold the commodity on the floor of the Memphis Cotton Exchange. By the end of the nineteenth century the production of hardwood lumber became Memphis' second major industry. In 1925 there were forty mills in the city producing three hundred million feet of lumber. The division of labor in these two industries closely matched the racial dynamics of Memphis. Most unskilled workers were African American while skilled workers, managers and owners were White. Commercial and civic leaders maintained this exploitation by keeping taxes and wages low while discouraging unskilled workers from unionizing.[5]

While exploitation flourished, the first steps toward economic creativity took place in 1846 when Memphis was chosen to be the western hub of a railroad line connecting the Atlantic Ocean with the Mississippi River. City government invested $500,000 in the Memphis and Charleston Railroad, which was completed in 1857. The railroad expanded the city's connections with western and European markets and established Memphis as an important port of international trade. The same year the Memphis & Charleston Railroad began operations, another rail line stretching from Memphis to Grenada, Mississippi, was built. In 1860 the Memphis & Ohio railroad connected with the Louisville & Nashville - providing Memphis with even more commercial markets in north Mississippi, Kentucky and middle Tennessee. After the Civil War, the Memphis & Paducah was built and became part of the Illinois Central Railroad System in 1896.

A railroad connecting Memphis with Little Rock, Arkansas, was completed in 1871 despite the obstacle of the Mississippi River. In order to overcome this natural barrier, goods and passengers were ferried across the river where they boarded another train for Little Rock. By 1890, ten railroads serviced Memphis with an average of fifty-two trains passing daily through the city. However, the Mississippi River remained an obstacle to growth until the Great Bridge at Memphis was completed in 1892. The third-longest bridge in the world at that time, it became known as the Frisco when the St. Louis-San Francisco Railway purchased the three-span steel-truss bridge in 1903. Memphis' position as a transportation hub increased when the Illinois Central Railroad constructed the two-track Harahan Bridge in 1916. Many national business leaders saw Memphis as ripe for investment. A St. Louis banker declared the city was "the Imperial City of the South....We want to invest our money in Memphis."[6]

A few industrial concerns took advantage of Memphis' distribution network to build plants in the area - in 1912 the Ford Motor Company located an assembly line in the city. Other industries soon followed, including Firestone Tire and Rubber and Standard Oil Company. However, cotton and lumber so dominated the market that despite its considerable transportation network, Memphis did not attract as many heavy industries as civic leaders hoped. According to historian Robert Sigafoos:

"Outsiders could not visualize the city as an industrial city like St. Louis, Birmingham, Louisville, or Cincinnati." Fortunately for Memphis other creative industries emerged that in the long-run would have a profound effect on the local economy.[7]

By the end of the nineteenth century Memphis had a thriving music scene. Professional musicians performed on riverboats and played in Beale Street gambling dens, houses of prostitution as well as the Grand Opera House and other local theaters. When Blues composer William Christopher Handy relocated to Memphis in 1907 he did so in part because the city had a large pool of trained performers who could play his compositions. The popularity of Handy's "Beale Street Blues," "Memphis Blues," and "St. Louis Blues" inspired some to abandon the exploitative economy and take up music.

African American laborer Will Shade formed the Memphis Jug Band in the early 1920s and they performed in the clubs on Beale Street as well as political rallies and social events throughout the city. In the mid-1920s Ralph Peer of the Victor Recording Company was in Memphis where he saw the group perform and was impressed with what he heard. Quickly signing them to a contract, their first recording session took place on February 24, 1927, at the McCall Building. Shade combined White European string music with African American musical traditions to create a new sound. In 1928 they were joined by house painter Charlie Burse who, along with Shade, honed the Memphis Jug Band style that exploded in popularity and led to the recording of several other jug bands, most notably Gus Cannon's Jug Stompers. The music of Will Shade, Charlie Burse, and Gus Cannon further expanded the creative economy by deepening Memphis' reputation as a musical center.[8]

This reputation attracted many others to Memphis, including Alabama native Sam Phillips who opened his Memphis Recording Service at 706 Union Avenue in 1950. Phillips believed that music could overcome the South's poverty and racism by giving the region's despised minority an opportunity to express their humanity. Phillips recorded Jackie Brenston and Ike Turner in 1951, and when their single "Rocket 88" was released by Chess records and became a popular hit, Phillips formed his own label called Sun Records. There he recorded many African American rhythm and blues artists, including furniture maker Rufus Thomas and truck driver B. B. King. Phillips also recorded White artists — most famously truck driver

Elvis Presley, tire builder Bill Black, and dry-cleaning worker Scotty Moore, who fused different musical styles into a new rollicking sound made up of equal parts country, rhythm and blues, jazz and popular ballads. They may not have known it, but Elvis, Scotty, and Bill were carrying forward a musical style started by Will Shade and his Memphis Jug Band thirty years before. Phillips also recorded such White artists as Johnny Cash, Jerry Lee Lewis, and Carl Perkins which solidified Memphis' position as the birthplace of rock 'n' roll music.[9]

Stax Records, founded by the brother-and-sister duo Jim Stewart and Estelle Axton, also contributed much to the city's creative economy. Located in South Memphis at the intersection of College and McLemore, Stax recorded Carla and Rufus Thomas, the Bar-Kays, Booker T. & the MGs, Eddie Floyd, Wilson Pickett, Otis Redding, Sam and Dave, the Staple Singers, and Isaac Hayes. The many seminal recordings that took place in Memphis should have made the Bluff City one of the nation's leading recording centers; however, several factors prevented this from happening. First, innovators like Sam Phillips, Jim Stewart and Estelle Axton, not to mention the musicians themselves, were unable to conform to the national recording company's corporate culture. Secondly, many of these same corporations already had a presence in nearby Nashville. In addition, leaders of the exploitative economy preferred to invest in the city's distribution and transportation network rather than an art form widely viewed by the city's White elite as worthless.[10]

It was not until Elvis Presley died in 1977 that the civic elite realized that Memphis' musical heritage could be exploited for economic gain. As tens of thousands of Elvis fans poured into Memphis each summer, the city began to invest in its tourism infrastructure. During the 1980s and 1990s the Beale Street Entertainment District, Graceland, the National Civil Rights Museum, and several other attractions created one of the city's most significant industries. According to the Memphis Convention and Visitors Bureau, 11.7 million tourists visited Memphis in 2017 where they spent $3.5 billion.[11]

Other forms of creativity also influenced the Memphis economy in the twentieth century. In 1916 Clarence Saunders opened his first self-service grocery store which allowed consumers to choose their own products rather than rely on clerks to provide them. The shopping public quickly embraced self-service. By 1921 there were 615 Piggly Wiggly stores in forty states with combined sales of $60 million.

Like Clarence Saunders, Memphian Kemmons Wilson also revolutionized an American industry. After finding it difficult to find acceptable lodgings during a family vacation, Wilson developed his Holiday Inn hotel chain in 1952. Holiday Inn offered several innovations that transformed the hotel experience in America, including ice machines, swimming pools, and a television set and telephones in each room. By 1969 there were 1,713 Holiday Inns across the country with gross sales of $404 million.

A vibrant and creative medical community was also located in Memphis, which stabilized and strengthened the local economy. Led by the University of Tennessee medical school, many local researchers contributed to the fields of bacteriology, cardiology, dentistry, and orthopedics. In 1962 entertainer Danny Thomas founded St. Jude's Children's Research Hospital which further established Memphis as one of the nation's top medical communities.[12]

On April 17, 1973, Federal Express launched its overnight package delivery service at the Memphis International Airport. Founded by Frederick W. Smith in Little Rock, Arkansas, in June 1972, the company relocated its headquarters to take advantage of the Bluff City's central location, superior airport facilities, and growing warehouse industry. Employing 389 workers and fourteen jet planes, the company delivered 186 packages to twenty-five cities during its first night of operation. A month later Federal Express purchased eighteen additional aircraft and in August they began a $2.9 million construction project to build aircraft hangers, a package-sorting facility, and permanent headquarters at the airport. In 2018 FedEx shipped 14 million packages per day which earned the company $65.5 billion in revenue globally and employed 33,000 Memphians.[13]

In order to expand the city's river and rail network Memphis secured $17 million from the federal Flood Control Act of 1946 to construct an industrial harbor on President's Island directly across from downtown. Opened in 1955, the harbor attracted many large companies including Sinclair Refining, Cargill, Mid-South Chemical, and Commercial Barge Lines, Inc. who took advantage of the area's combination river-rail-truck terminal and 7,800 acres of available storage space. The industrial harbor continued to grow well into the twenty-first century. In 2014 the harbor contained 135 businesses that employed 20,000 people, and handled 14.7 million tons of freight. By 2018 it was the nation's fifth-largest inland port.[14]

The Industrial Harbor and FedEx spawned a dramatic increase in the number of warehouses dotting the Memphis landscape. In the fall of 1972 Belz Investment Company had seven million square feet of warehouse space rented in Memphis and Wilkinson & Snowden, Inc. had six million. By 2014 there were 215.4 million square feet of occupied warehouse space in Memphis.

At the same time Memphis experienced a savage decline in its industrial base - Ford Motor Company, Firestone, and International Harvester closed, leaving well-paid, skilled workers without employment. As the University of Memphis's Bureau of Business & Economic Research reported in 1982, manufacturing was in decline because the city was "undergoing basic changes in its industrial structure."[15] Many skilled workers moved into the distribution business. Some remained in skilled positions, but others were forced to accept employment working on warehouse floors where wages were often low and working conditions poor. It is not much of an exaggeration to declare the warehouse to be the twenty-first century version of the cotton gin and compress plant - a place where unskilled workers endure exploitation for little pay. Perhaps the best example of this exploitation took place in October 2017 when a fifty-eight-year-old woman died of cardiac arrest while working in a warehouse shipping cell phones and tablets to consumers across the United States. In a horrific decision highlighting their suffering, managers ordered remaining employees to ignore the dead body sprawled on the warehouse floor and get back to work. At this same location several pregnant workers suffered miscarriages as a result of loading heavy boxes on conveyor belts in temperatures that often reached 100 degrees. Despite these macabre stories, companies still continue to build warehouses and Memphians still continue to work there. Amazon announced in September 2018 that it plans to locate a pair of distribution centers in Memphis that will employ fifteen hundred people.[16]

This is not to say that economic creativity has disappeared from the Bluff City. In fact, its culture of innovation continues to attract entrepreneurs to Memphis. In December 2018 for example, the high-tech agricultural firm Indigo Ag announced it was moving its headquarters from Boston to downtown Memphis. Company CEO David Perry explained that "Memphis has a great history of being an agricultural center, so that attracted us here. We're big in cotton and obviously [Memphis has] the Cotton Exchange. There's an enormous history with cotton in Memphis. And then we found a real connection between our core values as a company and Memphis. A great, pro-business environment.'' Memphis is also home to three Fortune 500 companies: AutoZone, FedEx, and International Paper, and two Fortune 1000 companies: Mueller Industries and ServiceMaster.[17]

As of 2019, the Bluff City has taken several important steps to improve the economic life of the city. In addition to attracting such important companies as Indigo Ag, Memphis has recently de-annexed several out-lying neighborhoods which has freed up tax dollars for use in the city's inner core. In addition, the city has become a national leader in adapting abandoned buildings and infrastructure for re-use. Yet too many of the old patterns persist - keeping large swaths of the citizenry trapped in low-wage jobs, living in sub-standard neighborhoods, and their children attending poor-performing schools. It remains to be seen whether Memphis can expand its creativity while eliminating the exploitation that has plagued the city for two hundred years.

CHAPTER EIGHT

MEMPHIS SOUNDS: HOW MUSIC SHAPED OUR CITY AND CHANGED THE WORLD

Charles L. Hughes

There are few things more associated with Memphis than its music. The city's importance to musical history includes legendary artists, crucial stylistic innovations, and a wealth of important and successful recordings that helped structure the soundtrack of the twentieth and twenty-first centuries. From blues to trap, Memphis' musicians and studios have become world-famous for their talents and made "Memphis" a marker of quality and authenticity for listeners around the world. Music has also become central to our city's identity. Music has fueled our growth, bolstered our economy, and bolstered our international reputation, making places like Beale Street and Sun Studios into sacred spaces for music lovers around the world. The sounds produced in Memphis have become pivotal to the stories we tell about the city's development and change.

Most significantly, music remains a favorite metaphor for the city's cherished identity as a social and cultural crossroads. Genres like rock 'n' roll and soul, or artists from B.B. King to Elvis Presley to Justin Timberlake, remain key symbols for the collisions that have defined the region's history and produced its distinctive sounds. The city's role as a regional center of migration and its storied history of Black-White musical overlap make such narratives both expected and justified.

But many of these narratives serve to bathe the story of Memphis music in a comforting nostalgia. As tourist campaigns herald the blues, rock 'n' roll, and soul music of yesteryear as a musically authentic and culturally positive force for good, the stories told about Memphis music implicitly (and sometimes explicitly) serve to affirm the idea that the old sounds and even the old days were better. As a song in the 2014 documentary *Take Me To The River* suggested, Memphis music urges us "to get it back where it's supposed to be."[1] But Memphis music has always been at its best – and among the world's best – when it does the opposite. The "Memphis sound" is a sonic confrontation of changing circumstances, with artists engaging moments of promise and peril, and listeners using music to express and process these changes. This process is as deep, funky, and compelling as the music itself.

From the beginning, Memphis' White founders saw the city as a potential capital of world culture alongside its economic centrality to the growing Cotton Kingdom. Motivated by the mixture of ambition and violence that characterized American expansion, the founders constructed the early city to include performance venues that would attract the world's great performers – like Swedish soprano Jenny Lind, who visited the city in 1851 – and promote the growth of a local arts community. But those who existed on Memphis' margins – poor Whites, European immigrants, and African Americans both free and enslaved – imported their own musical traditions and created their own innovative blends. It is that music, made by those whom Wanda Rushing notes were considered "of little substance" by city elites, that came to define the city's soundtrack.[2]

Of course, the first music in this region came from those who were here even before American settlement. Before the city's founding, the Chickasaws and other indigenous nations produced sounds for celebration and recreation that formed the area's first musical culture. As in other aspects of the city's history, these early echoes often get lost in considerations and commemorations. But we must acknowledge and honor this music and those who made it.

As the city grew, Black music became most significant in the mix. This coincided with the larger importance of African Americans to the city's development after the Civil War. In the years after Emancipation, Black people came to the city to enjoy the new opportunities of freedom created by the new infrastructure of Reconstruction and the city's pre-existing free Black community. In churches, parlors, meeting houses, bars, and other spaces, Black Memphians helped bridge the sounds of the past with the possibilities of the present.

The most famous of these spaces was Beale Street, the emergence of which at the turn of the twentieth century reflected both the tightening of Jim Crow restrictions and continued Black resilience. Among its multifaceted demonstration of Black power and accomplishment, Beale Street became a center of musical culture.[3] Its venues nurtured local and regional talent, as well as attracting an array of national touring stars for whom Memphis became a key stop on the national circuit. The glittering theatres and grooving nightclubs of Beale Street offered a place for Black

Memphians to develop a unique local scene and to participate — as both listeners and musicians — within the growing world of Black popular music in the twentieth century.

Beale Street became famous within that world in part because of the work of W.C. Handy. Like others of his time, Handy, who arrived in the early 1900s, hoped to marry older styles with the new sounds of an advancing and urbanizing Black population. Handy recalled learning the blues from an itinerant acoustic musician in Mississippi, an apocryphal story that nonetheless symbolizes his synthesis of those traditions with the marching music and orchestral arrangements that he embraced as both composer and conductor. In compositions like "Beale Street Blues" and "Memphis Blues," Handy celebrated his adopted community as a crucial demonstration of those larger shifts. Handy's fame skyrocketed; his compositions were performed around the world and he became a local celebrity. (He even earned a gig from Mayor Edward Hull Crump, who commissioned Handy to compose a campaign song for him.) His later self-anointing as the "Father of the Blues" is dubious, and he was far from Beale Street's sole catalyst, but W.C. Handy earned his enduring reputation as one of Memphis' key musical ambassadors.[4]

Handy symbolizes the larger efforts of Black musicians in the early decades of the twentieth century to simultaneously engage with tradition, break from minstrel-era stereotypes, and ring the changes of a new century. On Beale Street and elsewhere, Black Memphians — both longtime residents and recent arrivals — played a crucial role in those experiments. Sometimes the hybrids trended toward the funky Delta strut of guitar-slinging Memphis Minnie, while sometimes they luxuriated in the sparkling torch songs of Bessie Smith, who performed in Memphis and covered Handy's songs. Sometimes they sounded like the jug-band jump of the Beale Street Sheiks, and sometimes they recalled the uptown swing of Phineas Newborn and his family. They were on stage in the "Amateur Night" performances that created space for the city's talented Black youth, and in the long-running bands that supported the careers of generations of players.

The segregated landscape of Jim Crow Memphis nurtured rich networks of listenership, professional development, and artistic innovations. Segregated Black high schools, particularly Manassas and Booker T. Washington, produced young players and singers who pioneered the city's jazz and R&B sounds.[5] Churches and other sacred spaces nurtured the development of Memphis' contributions to Black gospel, including local luminaries like Rev. W.H. Brewster and Lucie Campbell, and made space for visiting stars like Mahalia Jackson and Sister Rosetta Tharpe. And the development of WDIA, the first all-Black radio station in the United States, amplified the musical talent of Black Memphis on the increasingly crowded airwaves. These institutions (and at least some of their White counterparts) helped produce the talent pool and larger infrastructure for the rock 'n' roll and R&B/soul revolutions to follow. As Rufus Thomas suggested, "Memphis' amateurs are the world's professionals."[6]

Those amateurs became professionals in a moment of significant change for Memphis' larger economic and political landscape. New industries (accompanied by the decline of the agricultural economy) brought thousands of new arrivals to the city. Many of them were attracted to the city at least in part because of its reputation as a music center, carried into the city on the sounds of the radio and the promise of musical opportunities. A new generation of Black activists pushed their predecessors to subvert the structures of Jim Crow more forcefully. And a growing number of White youth resisted the cultural expectations of their forbears.

As before, music became one of the most visible expressions of these changes. One individual who recognized and hoped to exploit this was Sam Phillips, who arrived in Memphis from Alabama and worked at several radio stations before opening the Memphis Recording Service in 1950.[7] Phillips' original vision for the business — and the record label, Sun Records, which emerged from it — was to document the music made by the city's Black musicians on Beale Street and elsewhere. Phillips was not the first person to attempt this. But he distinguished himself through his keen ear for talent and a desire to capture the unvarnished sounds emerging from the city's nightclubs. Armed with a unique artistic vision and network of contacts, Phillips recorded many of Memphis' Black musical luminaries of the period. He was the first to release cuts by Howlin' Wolf and B.B. King, scored hits from Beale Street regulars Rufus Thomas and Roscoe Gordon, and branched out to the vocal pop of The Prisonaires and the boogie stomp of Jackie Brenston and his Delta Cats, whose "Rocket 88" is sometimes cited as the first rock 'n' roll record.

Brenston's seeming sonic prophecy signaled a change at Sun that began with the arrival of a young musician in 1953. Elvis Presley came to the Memphis Recording Service because of the studio's growing reputation and his personal desire to become a recording artist.[8] There, he encountered studio manager Marion Keisker, who played a pivotal and underappreciated role in Sun's rise and became a champion for Presley in his early days. Presley's famous declaration to Keisker — "I don't sound like nobody" — came to define the youthful alchemy that characterized Presley's work. Most obviously a blend of country and blues, but with heavy shadings of gospel and pop, Presley's work at Sun Records galvanized a larger movement of white "rockabilly" artists and became a key sparkplug in the rock 'n' roll revolution of the 1950s.

The rockabilly artists at Sun Records joined counterparts in Chicago, New Orleans, and other cities in pioneering the exciting new sound and challenging cultural barriers in the civil rights era. With its cross-racial sound and interracial fan base, rock 'n' roll challenged racial boundaries at the dawn of the civil rights movement. The androgyny and overt sexuality of rock 'n' roll artists and fans accompanied the disruptions of the Sexual Revolution. The music's broader resonance as an uncontained expression of youth rebellion marked it as a site of anxiety and excitement in Cold War America. Memphis — the home of rock 'n' roll's biggest star — became a shorthand for both fans and opponents.

But Memphis' rock 'n' roll moment also assured its continuing role in historical debates over racial appropriation. While Elvis Presley himself was quick to cite his Black influences and praise his Black contemporaries, his rise as the White "king" of rock 'n' roll reinforced the notion that Black folks were being denied both the cultural and economic benefits of a music that they had created. Perhaps the most damning evidence for this was the fact that, in the aftermath of Presley's success, Sam Phillips stopped recording Black artists at Sun Records in favor of talented White musicians who drew on Black musical lineages. Even as it established Memphis as a rock 'n' roll capital and launched the careers of Jerry Lee Lewis, Johnny Cash, and other white stars, Phillips' move drew criticism from some of his Black artists and tainted his legacy as a figure of cultural boundary-busting. By establishing both possibilities and limitations, Sun set the stage for the city's next great musical revolution.

That revolution was centered at Stax Records, which opened in 1957 as an explicit attempt to capitalize on Sun's success.[9] Label co-owner Jim Stewart began his career as a country musician and hoped to find the next Elvis Presley. But, following the advice of his sister and co-owner

Estelle Axton, Stewart and company shifted their focus to the young Black talent that congregated around the new company's headquarters in South Memphis. This inversion of Sun's racial trajectory drew Black players ranging from high-school prodigy Booker T. Jones to elder statesmen Rufus Thomas, who brought his daughter Carla with him to the fledgling studio. This consolidation of talent helped Stax re-establish Memphis as a home of Black music, rather than White music that bore Black influence.

Stax became the primary label associated with the spare, funky music that became internationally known as Memphis soul. The success of homegrown artists like Rufus and Carla Thomas and imported talent like Sam & Dave and Otis Redding established Stax and the "Memphis sound" as part of soul music's emergence in the mid-1960s. Soul not only represented an exciting new sound but also formed the soundtrack to the assertive celebrations of the civil rights movement. With its deep grooves and interracial personnel, Stax became heralded as a symbol of soul progress and racial integration. In particular, the label's primary house band — the interracial combo Booker T. & the MGs — symbolized Stax's breakthrough commitment to cross-racial collaboration as both a musical framework and social project. Integration at Stax had its limits — the label's racial politics were complicated from the beginning, and Black artists sometimes registered complaints about the studio's practices. But the label's association with civil rights politics only strengthened after the killing of Dr. Martin Luther King Jr.

This cataclysm, particularly when combined with the death of Otis Redding a year earlier and the loss of the label's national distribution contract with Atlantic Records, shook Stax as a commercial entity and a cultural force. Nonetheless, the label surged after 1968, a demonstration of both its resilience and its renewed commitment to the cause of Black freedom both locally and nationally. Under the leadership of new president Al Bell, Stax allied itself with Freedom Movement causes ranging from Rev. Jesse Jackson's Operation PUSH to local concerns like the killing of Elton Hayes by Memphis police. Bell pushed for more Black front-office staff at Stax and challenged the larger industry's racial hierarchies. Stax also amplified the sonic and visual connections to the Black freedom struggle in work by the Staple Singers, Isaac Hayes, the Bar-Kays, and others. With massive successes like Hayes' Oscar-winning *Shaft* soundtrack and the 1972 *Wattstax* concert, Stax in the Al Bell years represented both a continuation of soul's promise and a new place for Memphis within it.

Stax's success propelled Memphis into an unprecedented era of recording success. At American Studios, producer Chips Moman and a talented house band worked with a wide variety of artists. American came to specialize particularly in White artists – The Box Tops, Dusty Springfield, a returning Elvis Presley – who incorporated soul music into their hit-making sounds. Al Green, Ann Peebles, and others joined the soul conversation at Hi Records, based out of Royal Studios and built around producer Willie Mitchell and the musicians known as Hi Rhythm. Ardent Studios specialized in White rock and pop – including Big Star – that bridged into the psychedelic '60s and the hard-rock '70s. The success of these studios (and others) gave Memphis a new level of prominence within the U.S. music industry and became part of the city's public-relations strategy in the tumultuous aftermath of the King assassination.

Unfortunately, the success was not to last. Stax Records closed in 1975 under ambiguous circumstances. While the reasons for this are still debated, its closure was not – as is sometimes suggested – a consequence of the King assassination or Black Power assertions. Instead, the label's end paralleled a wave of job loss and "White flight" demographic shifts that particularly affected the city's Black communities. Additionally, Stax's closing accompanied and fueled a larger downturn in the city's recording industry only a few years after its moment of greatest prominence. Sam Phillips retired, Chips Moman moved to Nashville, Beale Street was torn down as part of an "urban renewal" project, and Elvis Presley died at Graceland in 1977.

In the aftermath, many of its most successful music scenes offered a commentary on the musical past. The soul success of Hi Records continued into funk and disco, until Al Green left in the early 1980s to minister at his newly-opened Full Gospel Tabernacle in Whitehaven, not far from Graceland. Memphis' punk rock offered a joyous deconstruction. In venues like the Antenna Club, Alex Chilton broke apart the R&B and pop of his earlier bands the Box Tops and Big Star, Tav Falco exploded rockabilly and blues, and The Klitz claimed space for women.[10] Memphis punks failed to achieve the national notoriety of their New York or Los Angeles counterparts, but artists like The Oblivians, Pezz, and Jay Reatard extended the musical collisions into a new century.

The most significant musical reckoning took place in hip-hop. As Zandria F. Robinson describes, Memphis rap offered a "post-soul" soundtrack for "the intersection of the postindustrial conditions of unemployment and urban disinvestment, post-civil rights youth cultures, the reassertion of the South as a culturally, historically, and in some cases economically distinctive American region, and this history of fused musical genres and cultures."[11] The spare, bluesy parables by pioneers like Gangsta Pat and later stars like Three 6 Mafia expressed the desires and demands of a new generation of Black youth whose experience was informed, but not transcended, by previous eras or other scenes. Memphis became a key player in the "Dirty South" transformation of hip-hop as it entered a new century. (Three 6 Mafia even won an Oscar for "It's Hard Out Here For A Pimp," the theme song to the Memphis-themed film *Hustle & Flow.*) From Yo Gotti's street-corner symphonies to Al Kapone's history lessons to Gangsta Boo's pulsing assertions, Memphis hip-hop, both commercial and underground, remains a cornerstone of the city's local soundtrack and international reverberations.

Despite this, hip-hop remains on the margins of many narratives of Memphis music. Even as the city's best music remixed the traditions in new directions, Memphis' larger civic project sought to enshrine the "Memphis sound" in the past. Beale Street was rebuilt as a tourist site in the 1980s, at the same moment that Graceland arose as the centerpiece of the city's tourist economy. W.C. Handy's home and Sun Studios reopened as tourist sites, the Smithsonian Institution launched a music museum in Memphis, and both the Blues Hall of Fame and Memphis Music Hall of Fame opened and expanded. In perhaps the most powerful example, the Stax Museum of American Soul Music opened on the site of the now-demolished former studio alongside a music academy and charter school, reflecting the label's long interest in celebrating and supporting its South Memphis neighborhood. These acts of reclamation thankfully preserved and deservedly celebrated chapters in Memphis' history and impact on the world.

But this process of memorialization has also reinforced a narrative that locates Memphis' musical impact in a distant and sometimes mythological past. This not only shapes the work of contemporary Memphis musicians — who must fend with the weight of the city's musical legacies — but also has insidious effects on historical memory. Perhaps the most significant aspect concerns the city's storied history of Black and White musical overlap. In too many tenacious narratives, genres like rock 'n' roll or soul, or places like

Sun or Stax, get presented as transcendent places where race did not matter or did not even exist. While music created important spaces for interracial collaboration, such a narrative diminishes the critiques of Black musicians, overemphasizes the role of White collaborators and turns Memphis music into an ahistorical colorblind dreamland.[12]

This mythology holds real political value. It conveniently exists before the rise of Black Power and hip-hop. It renders invisible the larger structural inequities caused by deindustrialization, "White flight," disparities in policing or other factors that offer a rumbling counterpoint to the city's boosterism. Most specifically, it allows for the continued misapprehension that music (or arts more generally) somehow exist outside of the racial structures that dominate the rest of life in Memphis and the United States. This is neither true nor reflective of the actual history. Too often, Memphis musical nostalgia gets weaponized in the service of comforting fictions that gloss over the complexities of the past and preclude the honest assessments that are necessary for a more just future.

Given this tension, it is unsurprising that many of today's best Memphis musicians are engaging with the expectations of the past in dialogue with the opportunities of the present. Hip-hop continues to offer a voice for young Black Memphis in an age of demonization and marginalization. One particularly poignant example is Marco Pave's 2017 album *Welcome to Grc Lnd*, which juxtaposes civic fantasies with hard realities and includes accounts from #BlackLivesMatter activists arrested at a nonviolent protest in front of Graceland. Roots-rock collective Motel Mirrors recreates the crackling energy of Memphis rock 'n' roll without excessive reverence. Taliba Safiyah reconnects the city's jazz and soul legacies in a new century, while Valerie June links the mysteries of acoustic roots music with the magic of Bessie Smith and psychedelic rock. The children of the Memphis-Mississippi blues axis — Luther and Cody Dickinson, Cedric Burnside, Sharde Thomas, Steve Selvidge, and others — continue the conversation begun by their parents and predecessors. New voices in jazz, gospel, Latinx music, and other styles push the boundaries of Memphis' musical identity. Working musicians continue to play the changes on stages from Beale Street to the suburbs. Most importantly, perhaps, the next generation of musicians gather in spaces around the city to find their sounds and enter the conversation.

Now, as ever, the "Memphis sound" is an ongoing process more than a specific set of stylistic markers. Memphis' musicians and their audiences address a changing city by blending the sounds of the past with the possibilities and perils of the moment. Not content with safe nostalgia but deeply invested in its traditions, Memphis music remains a primary way of understanding this place and its people. As they always have, the musicians give us a guide. It's our obligation to keep listening.

CHAPTER NINE

THE SOUTH'S MOVEABLE FEAST:
FOOD IN MEMPHIS

Jennifer Biggs

From roughly 1850 to 1930, about twenty-five million European immigrants came to the shores of the United States. Ellis Island comes to mind as the first glimpse they saw of their new home, but it wasn't the only point of entry. Baltimore, San Francisco, Galveston, Philadelphia, and most important to Memphis — New Orleans — were among other ports. After a boat ride across the Atlantic, a shorter one up the Mississippi River was a small price to find a home in Memphis, a river town bustling with commerce when not suffering through yellow fever epidemics. They came, and with them they brought their food.

Rinaldo Grisanti came here and opened a restaurant on Main Street in 1909. There have been about a dozen Grisanti's restaurants — perhaps double that — over the years and today, four members of his family still operate vibrant restaurants: Ronnie Grisanti's, Frank Grisanti's, David Grisanti's and Dino's Grill. In 1919, Speros Zepatos opened The Arcade where it still stands today at the corner of South Main and G.E. Patterson; it's the oldest restaurant in town. Also from Greece like Zepatos, James Catsoodas opened Jim's Place Downtown, and soon was joined by brothers Nick and Bill Taras. Today, Dimitri Taras and his sons still own Jim's Place Grill in Collierville, where photographs of their ancestors hang in honor on the walls. Charlie Vergos opened a tavern and eventually decided to sell ribs there. The Rendezvous, which turned seventy-years old in 2018, is known all over the world today for its dry rub ribs and alley entrance, a destination for both locals and tourists.

Memphis clearly owes a culinary debt to these immigrants, but the city's location on the river, surrounded by fertile farmland, shaped a restaurant community that never had to utter the words "farm to table." It was simply always that way: grow it, cook it, eat it.

But going way back, long before the immigrant restaurateurs, before the country cooks who would come to the city bringing the home cooking and soul food to restaurants around town, even before the farmers,

Memphis and the surrounding area were ground zero for what would become a food that would define not just us, but various regions of the American South. When Hernando de Soto headed north from Florida on his quest to claim land for Spain, he and his conquistadors traveled with pigs. In winter 1540, de Soto and his men made camp with the Chickasaw Indians near Tupelo, Mississippi, about one hundred miles south of town.[1] There's a record of a pig roast with the Indians there, close to five hundred years ago. When de Soto and his men moved on, many of the pigs that had been left to forage in the forest stayed and they multiplied. This introduction of pigs gives award-winning author Adrian Miller fodder to support the claim that barbecue as we know it originated in the Memphis area. Texas claims it — but cooks beef barbecue. Miller contends that pork is the original American barbecue. The Carolinas call it their own, but if pigs were here first, well, there's that. As for Kansas City, ditto.

On Delta plantations, pigs were raised for food, and barbecue was to political stumping what fish fries are today. By 1910, advertisements for barbecue were seen in local newspapers, according to Miller, and we know that in 1922, Leonard Heuberger opened shop at Trigg and Latham in South Memphis, where he sold pork sandwiches for five cents. About ten years later, he moved to what Memphians mostly think of as the original Leonard's at Bellevue and McLemore. Leonard's is now owned by Dan Brown, who started working for Mr. Heuberger in 1962, and in 1993 bought the company from a group of investors that had big plans to expand it nationally. Today there's one location left in East Memphis.

Barbecue is important to Memphis and has brought international recognition to the city. Kemmons Wilson, the founder of Holiday Inn, took guests from all over the world to the Rendezvous. Jim Neely, who owns Interstate Bar-B-Que, trained his children and nephews who went on to star in the Food Network show "Down Home with the Neelys." One of Neely's favorite places to eat when he was younger was Brady & Lil's, a barbecue restaurant that was purchased in 1981 by Frank Vernon and eventually renamed the Bar-B-Q Shop. Brady Vincent invented barbecue spaghetti; Vernon perfected it, and no one else really knows how he makes it. Barbecue nachos are Memphis born, too. You can't patent them, so claims of who made them first, fly around, but good money says it was a woman named Rosie who worked for Walker Taylor's Germantown Commissary. She threw a handful on an order of chips and cheese sauce at an outdoor festival and an iconic dish was born. Some time between spaghetti and nachos, Horest Coletta was running a restaurant on South Parkway that his father opened as an ice cream parlor in the 1920s. After World War II, soldiers returned home with a taste for pizza (and for wine, but that's a different story) and Coletta obliged. To get locals interested in his pizza, he did what only a Memphian would do: he put barbecue on it, and thus the world received the gift of barbecue pizza.

While Memphis is more than barbecue — infinitely more — it is home to the Memphis in May World Championship Barbecue Cooking Contest. Kansas City makes noise about being the barbecue capital of the country, and that city's American Royal World Series of Barbecue® contest is twice the size of our annual event. But it must be noted that here we confine major competition to pork — remember, the original barbecue — and in Kansas City they have multiple categories.

While barbecue is part of who we are, it's not all. Memphis is a city of locally-owned restaurants that spread all over town and the suburbs. These places range from small mom and pops largely unknown outside their neighborhoods to upscale places manned by chefs who could work anywhere in the world and choose to ply their trade in Memphis. Master Chef Jose Gutierrez came to Memphis to take over the kitchen of Chez Philippe in The Peabody only a few months after it opened in the early 1980s, and shortly thereafter snagged a Food & Wine's Best New Chef award. He left after twenty-two years and is now chef/owner at River Oaks Restaurant in East Memphis. Two of his former cooks, Andy Ticer and Michael Hudman grabbed the same award in 2013, a few years after opening Andrew Michael Italian Kitchen, their first restaurant, and a few years after Restaurant Iris and The Second Line chef/owner Kelly English made the 2009 list. Four young chefs recognized as among the best of the in the country isn't a shabby claim for any city.

Gutierrez was among the first wave of chefs to put Memphis on the culinary map. In 1977, University of Memphis Track Coach Glenn Hays opened La Tourelle, a French restaurant that would bring talent to town and train young chefs. Erling Jensen was one of them. He answered an ad in The New York Times, talked to Hays by phone and soon rolled into town in a convertible with a Great Dane, took charge of the kitchen, and helped change fine dining in Memphis. Justine's was still around then, but other old fine dining restaurants were gone or on their way out. Jensen now owns Erling Jensen: The Restaurant and has trained numerous chefs who have gone on to make their mark with their own places. Justin Young worked there and now owns Raven & Lily and Jimmy Gentry has P.O. Press, both in Collierville; Dave Krog will open Dory mid-2019 in East Memphis. While this was going on — the La Tourelle days — in Memphis, KC's Kitchen in Cleveland, Mississippi, was turning out fine food and serving from a stellar wine cellar. Wally Joe, son of the owners, made his way to Memphis and now owns ACRE. Karen Carrier, a native Memphian who'd opened Automatic Slims in the meat-packing district in New York, came home and in the early 1990s opened a restaurant with the same name on Second Street downtown. She's since sold that to restaurateur Sandy Robertson, who owns Dyer's and Alfred's on Beale, and Carrier has Mollie Fontaine Lounge, Bar BKDC, and the Beauty Shop. By the turn of the new millennium, Memphis had reassembled a band of upper-end dining venues, and more were to come.

Always a place for soul food and home cooking restaurants — Four Way Grill opened in 1946 and The Cupboard in 1943 — Memphis was also diversifying its palate along with its population. Folks who had grown up eating in one of two Mexican restaurants in town (there were a few more, but you had to know where to find them) were eating in taquerias that dotted Summer Avenue. On Cleveland, Saigon Le was one of the early Vietnamese restaurants to line the street, only to burn down a few years ago. Yet it opened long after Lotus, which is still on Summer Avenue where it started in the late 1970s, still owned by Joe and Hanh Bach.

Some of the credit for this goes to Catholic Charities, which for years offered immigration services. Some of the draw to the city is because family or friends already had moved here and also to the relative low cost of living and opening a small business. Whatever the case, the 1990s and 2000s brought a new wave of immigrants that continue to enrich the city's food scene. Abyssinia was Memphis' first Ethiopian restaurant when it opened in 2000; today there are five in the city.

And there are at least three Colombian restaurants; two that serve Cuban food, and a couple that offer other Caribbean cuisine; two Venezuelan places; a dozen or more Indian restaurants; dozens of Japanese places from small to large; Middle Eastern food served by families that come from Yemen, Iraq, Jordan, Palestine, and other countries; pho is served in a dozen or so Vietnamese restaurants; Thai restaurants serve food so spicy it should come with a warning; authentic Chinese cuisine is found on the red menu, not the Americanized green one, in several restaurants; and there are more taco food trucks on the street than there were Mexican restaurants in the entire city about a decade ago.

Memphis hasn't escaped the long arm of the chains, but it abounds with chef-owned and family-owned restaurants and has a population loyal to locals. Where you eat old school Italian likely depends on where your parents ate: Pete & Sam's or Coletta's. The former recently marked its seventieth anniversary and the latter is coming up on one hundred years since the ice cream shop that became the restaurant opened. But even as folks stay true to the old, newer restaurants continue to change the dining landscape.

In 2008, Andy Ticer and Michael Hudman opened Andrew Michael Italian Kitchen on Brookhaven Circle in East Memphis. The childhood friends had a plan and have stuck with it. By the time they celebrated their tenth anniversary last year, they had four restaurants in Memphis and one in New Orleans: Hog & Hominy across the street from AMIK, Catherine & Mary's and The Gray Canary in downtown Memphis, and Josephine Estelle in the Ace Hotel in New Orleans.

That same year Kelly English opened Restaurant Iris and later followed with The Second Line. It was also the year that local baker Kat Gordon opened Muddy's Bake Shop. This crop of new business owners were all in their twenties. They're still cooking, still expanding, still winning awards, and gaining national, even international recognition, despite opening in a year that was financially devastating to businesses all around the country.

It's not surprising, looking at the history of Memphis' entrepreneurial spirit in the food business. It was here that the supermarket was born. Clarence Saunders opened Piggly Wiggly, the first self-serve grocery, in 1916. Before he lost ownership of it in a stock market deal in 1923, it had grown to almost thirteen hundred stores, about half his and half franchises. Saunders also lost the home he was building, now the Pink Palace Museum, in the same deal. Ronco Foods, founded by Italian immigrants in 1929, was once the largest manufacturer of pasta in the country.

While Fred Smith is a household name, the FedEx founder's father, also Fred Smith, started a business long before his son. The elder Smith was the owner of a chain of diners named Toddle House. He sold the chain in 1962 to Memphis-based Dobbs House, but when he owned them, Toddle

House restaurants were operated on an honor system: you deposited your check and your money in a glass case as you left.

Big John Grisanti, a colorful member of the family mentioned above and father of David, who owns David Grisanti's restaurant, held two world records for purchasing the most expensive bottles of wines in the late 1970s and early 1980s. One was a jeroboam of Chateau Lafite Rothschild 1864, for which he paid $18,000. The other was a $31,000 bottle of Lafite 1822. But he barely tasted them. Instead he did what a big-hearted, true Memphian would do: he auctioned sips of the wines to raise money for St. Jude Children's Research Hospital. This generosity of spirit – sharing food together – has been a part of Memphis from its beginnings.

CHAPTER TEN

A BRIEF HISTORY OF RELIGION IN MEMPHIS

David Waters

As the twentieth century dawned, Charles Harrison Mason was just another "colored" peasant in King Cotton's Delta. Robert Greene Lee was just another White plowboy in Jim Crow's Dixie. Lucie Eddie Campbell was just another elementary teacher in a Negro school in Boss Crump's Memphis. James Aaron Wax was just a Jewish kid upriver in a little Missouri town called Herculaneum. Over the course of the next fifty years, each would make an indelible mark on the religious history of Memphis, America, and the world.

It's no wonder. The history of religion in Memphis is personal and political, powerful and prolific. It oppressed and rescued, inspired and incited the sacred and the secular. Like money in New York, power in Washington, and fame in Hollywood, religion in Memphis informed just about everything that has happened here, from where we live and work and send our kids to school to how and why we eat, pray, love, hate, vote, sing and shout.

The first resident preacher in Memphis was a slave, a Methodist named Harry Lawrence, who began preaching to street-corner crowds of Whites and Blacks in 1822, three years after the city's founding. The city's first church also was Methodist. Members of First Methodist Church began gathering for worship in a log cabin at Poplar and Second in 1826.

That was decades before the South became known as the Bible Belt and Memphis was dubbed by some as its "buckle." Today, members of all major faiths and denominations can find at least one place of worship in Memphis. According to Glenmary Research Center in Atlanta, nearly six hundred thousand people in Shelby County adhere to a particular religion.[1] The actual figure is probably even larger.

***

Memphis is headquarters to three Christian denominations — the Christian Methodist Episcopal Church, the Cumberland Presbyterian Church, and most notably, Mason's Church of God in Christ.

C.H. Mason, the Memphis-born son of former slaves, was a dirt-road revivalist whose controversial "holiness" preaching once landed him in jail in Mississippi. In 1907, Mason traveled to the now-historic 1907 Azusa Street Revival in Los Angeles where he was "slain in the spirit," baptized not with water by man but with fire by God. "That night, the Lord spoke to me that Jesus saw all of this world's wrongs but did not attempt to set it right until God overshadowed Him with the Holy Ghost," he reported.[2]

Mason returned to Memphis and reorganized his small holiness sect into the world's first Pentecostal denomination, the Church of God in Christ. The rest is a large part of the history of religion in the twentieth century. "What appeared to be an insignificant religious upheaval among some poor, obscure blacks in the Delta region of Mississippi would become, in fact, a major reorganization of the black church in America, and a major bearer of Pentecostal spirituality in the 20th Century," Bishop Ithiel Clemmons wrote in his history of the denomination.[3]

Today, the Memphis-based Church of God in Christ is one of the nation's largest and most influential denominations. The Assemblies of God, another denomination with Mid-South roots in Mason's church, is the fastest-growing body of Christian believers in the world. And the religious movement known as Pentecostalism now claims one in four Christians worldwide.

Bishop C. H. Mason's legacy extends far beyond the church walls. The Church of God in Christ played a significant role in the Great Migration of rural southern Blacks to large urban areas outside the South. Mason sent ministers to Chicago, Detroit, Los Angeles, and other major cities to start mission churches, which not only grew the church, but also helped African Americans adapt to new environments. Mason Temple, the denomination's Memphis headquarters, was the largest African American church building in the world when it opened in the 1940s. When Mason died in 1961, he was entombed in the temple. On April 3, 1968, Dr. Martin Luther King Jr. delivered his last sermon, the famous "Mountaintop" speech, inside Mason Temple.

"The Church of God in Christ story reminds us that Black people who migrated to the cities were economically poor but spiritually rich," Dr. Robert Franklin, a COGIC minister and seminary dean, wrote in *My Soul Says Yes*.[4] "It is a story of humanizing modern city life through spiritual renewal, economic empowerment, cultural preservation, collective resistance, and existential celebration."

***

Memphis is home to Pentecostals and Presbyterians, Methodists and Muslims, Mormons, Jews and Jains, Greek Orthodox, Chinese Baptists and Vietnamese Catholics, Bahai and Buddhists, and lots and lots of Baptists. In fact, one of five people of faith in Shelby County call themselves Baptists — and half of them Southern Baptists.

On Dec. 11, 1927, R. G. Lee, a sharecropper's son from South Carolina, preached his first sermon as pastor of a struggling Bellevue Baptist Church in Midtown Memphis. Lee's legend seemed to grow every time he gave his signature sermon, "Payday — Someday," which he delivered more than one thousand times. Dressed in his trademark white suit and shoes, the fiery Lee would raise his arms then drop to his knees: "To the individual who goes not the direction God wants, a terrible pay day comes," he'd say. "To the nation which forgets God, pay day will come in the awful realization of the truth that the nations which forget God shall be turned into hell."[5]

When Lee arrived, Bellevue had twelve hundred members and an account balance of $39.49. By the time he retired thirty-three years later, Bellevue's membership had grown to ninety-two hundred with annual receipts of $650,000. Under Lee's guidance, Bellevue became one of the largest and most influential congregations in the Southern Baptist Convention, the nation's largest and most influential Protestant denomination. Bellevue became the first church in the world to own its own television station.

Lee, who wrote fifty books, became "Mr. Southern Baptist." He was elected president of the Southern Baptist Convention in 1948, 1949, and 1950 - the only man elected to the post for three consecutive years.

His Biblical conservatism and unyielding convictions helped to set a course that eventually put the denomination in the hands of conservative leaders. When Lee died in 1978, Billy Graham, also a Southern Baptist, called the Memphis pastor, "one of the towering spiritual giants of this century... He was a great preacher, a great writer, and a great student of the word of God. He firmly stood for the truth of Christ, regardless of the opinions of others."[6]

Over the years, Bellevue's legendary senior pastors - R.G. Lee, Ramsey Pollard, Adrian Rogers, and Steve Gaines - have served ten terms as president of the Southern Baptist Convention and set the tone and the agenda for the nation's conservative Christians. Rogers was president for three terms, leading the ultraconservative realignment of the SBC. Because of Bellevue, Memphis was a hub of the Religious Right movement that transformed American politics from Reagan to Trump. In the late 1970s, Bellevue member Ed McAteer brought together political, cultural, financial, and religious conservatives such as Jerry Falwell, Pat Robertson, and Rogers. McAteer's Religious Roundtable begat the Moral Majority, the Christian Coalition, and other conservative political forces that pushed the Republican Party further to the right, especially on social issues.

***

Religion in Memphis informed the compassion of the Martyrs of Memphis, the Episcopal Sisters of St. Mary — Constance, Frances, Ruth, and Thecla — who died while nursing the poor, sick, and dying during the yellow fever epidemic of 1878. Faith informed the courage of Rev. Nancy Hastings Sehested, who in 1987 became the first woman to lead a Southern Baptist congregation here, and Rev. Gina M. Stewart, who in 1995 became the first woman to lead a Black Baptist congregation. Faith informed the conviction of Catholic Bishop Carroll Dozier, who became the first American bishop to publicly oppose the Vietnam War; Rev. Dr. Benjamin Hooks, who, in 1965, became the first Black judge in Tennessee and in 1977 was named executive director of the national NAACP; and Rabbi James Wax of Temple Israel.

It was a seminal moment in Memphis history, a rabbi confronting a Jewish-born mayor at a critical juncture in the Black civil rights movement. "There are laws greater than the laws of Memphis and Tennessee, and these are the laws of God," Rabbi Wax of Temple Israel told Mayor Henry Loeb on April 5, 1968.[7]

Wax's finger-pointing lecture to Loeb hours after the assassination of Dr. Martin Luther King Jr. was broadcast across the country. The scene captured the drama of the day, but also reflected similar and less publicized scenes played out on various stages for decades in Memphis and across the South. Southern rabbis, many born outside the United States and all too familiar with Old Testament slavery and modern genocide, were the first White clergy in their communities to speak out against segregation and Jim Crow.

Half a century before, Dr. William Fineshriber of the congregation that became Temple Israel, became the first local man to speak publicly in favor of women's suffrage. In 1917, he persuaded his congregation and about twenty other clergy to protest the public immolation of a Black man in Memphis. And in 1921, he publicly criticized the Ku Klux Klan in a series of sermons covered by *The Commercial Appeal*. The next year, C.P.J. Mooney, Fineshriber's friend and the newspaper's editor, began a front-page attack on the Klan that won a Pulitzer Prize. "Northern rabbis jeopardized their life by going to places like Birmingham and Selma," wrote the late Dr. Berkley Kalin of the University of Memphis. "But Southern rabbis like Fineshriber not only risked their own lives but also the lives of their family and congregations by speaking out."[8]

***

Religion in Memphis touched Pentecostal church singers, such as Elvis Presley, Johnny Cash, and Al Green, preachers' kids, such as Aretha Franklin and Kirk Whalum, and Southern gospel legends, such as W. Herbert Brewster, the Blackwood Brothers, and Lucie Campbell. Lucie E. Campbell, the youngest of nine siblings born to former slaves in Duck Hill, Mississippi, never knew her father, a railroad worker, who died on the job before she was born. Her mother moved the family to Memphis. Lucie taught herself to play the piano and graduated valedictorian of her 1899 class at what became Booker T. Washington High. She taught elementary school, then English and American history at her alma mater for more than four decades. She also taught America to love Black gospel music.

In 1916, Campbell became music director for the National Baptist Convention U.S.A. Inc., the largest Black denomination in America. She helped edit popular hymnals, including *Gospel Pearls*, the first black Baptist hymnal to include songs that would be known as gospel. As the denomination's music director, she introduced America to Thomas Dorsey, who wrote *"Take My Hand, Precious Lord,"* and is now known as the Father of Gospel Music; to Marian Anderson, later invited by President and Mrs. Roosevelt to sing at an Easter 1939 concert on the steps of the Lincoln Memorial; and to J. Robert Bradley, Dr. King's favorite singer. Campbell also composed more than one hundred gospel songs, including "He'll Understand and Say Well Done" and "Something Within." Mahalia Jackson, Sam Cooke, and Sister Rosetta Tharpe, "the Grandmother of Rock and Roll," turned some of her songs into hits. Campbell died in 1963 at 77. Lucie E. Campbell Elementary School in north Memphis is named for her.

***

Religion in Memphis has inspired the formation of countless nonprofit organizations, including Memphis Inter Faith Association (MIFA); BRIDGES, Streets Ministries, the Church Health Center, Christ Community Health Services, the Memphis Jewish Home, the Ave Maria Home, Wesley Senior Ministries, Hope Christian Community Foundation, Jewish Community Partners, and the Assisi Foundation. Religion in Memphis has helped to heal us at Baptist, Methodist, St. Joseph, Saint Francis, and St. Jude hospitals. It has educated us at Presbyterian Day School, Solomon Schechter Day School, Pleasant View School, Rhodes College, LeMoyne-Owen College, and Christian Brothers University, not to mention Memphis Theological Seminary, Mid-America Baptist Theological Seminary, Harding Graduate School of Religion, and the Bornblum Judaic Studies Department at University of Memphis.

Religion in Memphis erected the giant Bellevue crosses near Interstate 40, the Statue of Liberation through Christ in Hickory Hill, and the Memphis Buddha in Parkway Village. It converted a synagogue into a church, a church into a mosque, a movie theater into a Jehovah's Kingdom Hall. It built the solemn Mason Temple and the elegant Temple Israel complex, the remarkable Hindu Temple in Eads, the resplendent Buddhist Temple in Crosstown, the regal Mormon Temple in Bartlett, and hundreds of other brush arbors and chapels and cathedrals across the city. Most importantly, religion in Memphis built community. Its fathers and mothers, sons and daughters, leaders and followers have knitted us together in countless ways for generations.

Memphis, the ancient capital of the Egyptian Delta, was a regional center for commerce, trade, and religion for centuries. Its modern namesake, the capital of the American Delta, has become that as well. Religion was and will continue to be a vital element in the birth, growth, and development of Memphis.

CHAPTER ELEVEN

THE HOOKS BROTHERS OF MEMPHIS: ARTIST-PHOTOGRAPHERS OF THE "NEW NEGRO" MOVEMENT IN THE URBAN SOUTH

Earnestine Jenkins

Vintage, turn-of-the-century photographs of African Americans increasingly attract the attention of scholars, collectors, and cultural institutions. Deborah Willis, a leading scholar in American photography uses the phrase "New Negro aesthetic" to describe the phenomenon in American visual history when a newly freed people first possessed the power to construct their own image.[1] Willis defines a particular style of representation linked to the New Negro movement (sometimes known as the Harlem Renaissance), at the turn of the twentieth century that celebrated African American identity, history, arts, and culture. Photographers like James Van Der Zee in Harlem and Addison Scurlock in Washington, DC, achieved national acclaim because of their artistic and technical proficiency. Early Black photographers, in using the accessible medium and technology of photography, transformed the public image of Black Americans. In the process, they helped to "visualize" the concept of the "New Negro," a term first used in 1895 to explain the new twentieth-century spirit exemplified by political activity and racial pride.[2]

W.E.B. Du Bois described this as a liberation from the history of slavery and emancipation to pursue self-sufficiency and equity in American society.[3] He saw a role for the visual arts, especially in reference to photography, a medium that lent itself to the construction of images that portrayed Black people the way they wanted to be seen: new identities, new prospects, new job opportunities, and new lives. African American photographers and their subjects challenged the stereotypes that denied Black humanity. Photography documented African American artists, political leaders, educators, historians, lawyers, and philosophers, as well as the poor but self-reliant, the striving working class, and the emerging middle class. From this collective and collaborative cultural expression came forth images both radical and compelling. According to Willis, images of the "idealized self" or 'New Negro" depicted men and women who were proud of their race, and demanded full citizenship rights.

In Memphis, the Hooks Brothers were the equivalent of James Van Der Zee and Addison Scurlock. Comparable to other prominent Black photographers of their day, they made discernable the aspirations, hopes, and dreams of a people.[4] Their pictures of churches, church groups and conventions, students and schools, athletic teams and sports events, parades and street scenes, businesses and images of entrepreneurship captured the bustle of everyday Black life in the urban South. When African Americans in Memphis were drafted into war, soldiers did not leave before going down to the Hooks Brothers studio to have their portraits taken. The Hooks Brothers left a valuable record of the Black entertainment figures from the world of cinema and music, including gospel, jazz, and blues musicians. The collection also preserves a record of Black medical care, picturing the physicians, nurses, and hospitals that provided health care for the African American community in Memphis. The content documenting the Black community in Memphis was, therefore, quite diverse. The working class, middle class, and the poor, alongside the prominent, all make their appearance in Hooks Brothers' photographs. The Hooks Brothers were the most influential photographers of the first half of the twentieth century in Memphis and the Mid-South. They established the precedent for a thriving Black photographic tradition in the city. This chapter examines just a few of their early works, interpreting the beginning decades of an extraordinary career that endured for three quarters of a century.

MEMPHIS, W. E. B. DU BOIS AND THE 1900 PARIS EXPOSITION

Photography became indelibly linked to the New Negro movement following the 1900 Paris Exhibition organized by W. E. B. Du Bois.[5] In preparation for the 1900 Paris Exposition, Du Bois carefully amassed an awe-inspiring group of photographs intended to showcase African American achievements. The Black leadership class, businesses, and educational and cultural institutions rallied to his cause, as did a number of African American photographers like Thomas Askew of Atlanta. Du Bois carefully chose photographs that displayed the great diversity of skin color and physical features among Black Americans. About five hundred engaging images eventually comprised *The American Negro Exhibit*, successfully illustrating the accomplishments of the "race" since Emancipation.

Among the individuals who complied with Du Bois' request for images of outstanding homes was wealthy Memphis businessman Robert R. Church Sr.[6] Du Bois wanted a picture of Church's imposing residence at 384 Lauderdale Street, **(Fig.1)**. The 300 block of South Lauderdale was one of Memphis' older racially-integrated neighborhoods developed before 1900. According to his granddaughter, Roberta Church, this was a period when Whites did not flee to the suburbs in objection to neighbors of color.[7] Prominent White and Black leaders in the city lived within the 300-400 block radius of Lauderdale. The *Planters Journal* published a lengthy description of the Church home in 1906, proclaiming it "the finest and most modern dwelling owned by a colored man in this country."[8]

Church started construction on the house in 1884. It was a three-story home, and possibly the first Queen Anne style residence erected in Memphis. The fourteen rooms included a cellar, bathroom, butler's pantry, and storerooms. The impressive public rooms on the first floor featured a thirty-six by sixteen-feet double drawing room, reception and dining room, and a ten-foot hall that ran the entire length of a handsomely furnished parlor. Church hired an artist from Italy to paint murals on the walls.

The mansion was situated on a corner lot with a commanding view of Lauderdale and Vance streets. Church completed the home in time for his wedding to Miss Anna Wright in 1885. The *Memphis Daily Appeal* of January 1, 1885 commented at the end of its detailed announcement:

> No colored man is better known in Memphis than Bob Church...By energy and prompt attention he has shown to his race what possibilities are in store for them, as he has accumulated a fortune of nearly 100,000, and lives in luxurious ease, respected by all. Mr. Church will occupy the magnificent residence recently constructed by him, and with his new wife and intelligent daughter, recently graduated at Oberlin.[9]

The photograph of the exterior showcased the stables, stone walkway, and iron fence that enclosed the entire property. Similar to the Atlanta photographs by African American photographer Thomas Askew, the picture of Church's new-found wealth, as symbolized in his impressive home, highlighted the wide range of experiences available to the "New Negro." The image was representative of how African American

Fig.1 Home of R.R. Church, 1890-1900. Vance and Lauderdale
Displayed as part of the American Negro exhibit at the Paris Exposition of 1900.
Church Family Papers, Special Collections-University of Memphis

photographers were documenting middle-class prosperity and prominent race leaders of the new century around the country.

The Hooks Brothers were the leading photographers doing this work in Memphis. In *Beale Street Where the Blues Began*, (1934), author and political figure George W. Lee, describes the Hooks Brothers studio as "The oldest of the artist's studios, on Beale near Third," indicating that it had seen "the rise and decline of many ambitious ventures."[10] Robert and Henry Hooks opened their commercial photography studio on Beale in 1907. In 1908, they were featured in Green P. Hamilton's book, *The Brighter Side of Memphis*.[11] Hamilton, a prominent African American educator, wrote his book to challenge the negative stereotypes about the Black community in Memphis. His book can be situated within the context of a growing, influential Black print culture (books, magazines, newspapers), during the New Negro movement that sought to counteract the demoralizing images that permeated American culture.

Black print culture made extensive use of photographs including portraits and African American-owned homes, churches, and businesses. Hamilton's book likewise employed many photographs to make visible Black success and achievements in Memphis. He described the Hooks Brothers studio as one of the best in the region.[12]

"RACE" MEN AND THE POLITICS OF PHOTOGRAPHIC PORTRAITURE

Images of African American leaders involved in political and early civil rights work, like Booker T. Washington, were important models of emulation during the New Negro movement. In *Booker T. Washington and the Art of Self-Representation*, Michael Bieze explained how successful Washington was in manipulating his image by exploiting the photographic medium.[13] Washington's interests in photography's potential for representation informed his early appreciation for the arts and visual culture. In 1900, Washington published *A New Negro for a New Century: An Accurate and Up-to-Date Record of the Upward Struggles of the Negro Race,* a four hundred-page book that included sixty photographs of prominent Blacks in America.[14] When Washington established the photography department at Tuskegee Institute when he became leader there, it was the first of its kind at a historical Black college. Tuskegee became an important center for the development of an aesthetically pleasing style of photography centered on imaging its international celebrity figure as a world-class leader of culture and influence. Local African American photographers based in urban centers like Memphis were strongly impacted by the manner of representation validated by prominent race male leaders like Washington.

In Memphis, the undisputed African American political leader was Robert Church Jr. Church was friends with Washington and was one of the first to join Washington's National Negro Business League.[15] Church first achieved prominence as the businessman who inherited the family wealth of his father, Robert Church Sr. During the early twentieth century, he established himself as one of the most influential African American Republican leaders in the nation.[16] Church believed access to the ballot was the only hope minorities had for empowerment. His political career began when he served as a delegate from the Tenth Congressional District at the Republican National Convention in 1912. He served as delegate at the next seven conventions until 1940. At the height of his influence during the 1920s, Church controlled federal patronage in the Tenth Congressional District during the administrations of Republican presidents Warren G. Harding, Calvin Coolidge, and Herbert Hoover. While he was prohibited from appointing African Americans to public offices, he influenced the appointments of White representatives who might serve Black interests. Church was involved in the selection of a U. S. Attorney General for West Tennessee, two White federal judges, and several postmasters. He ensured that the Black vote in Memphis determined the outcome of two mayoral elections during the 1920s, resulting in the defeat of candidates with Ku Klux Klan membership seeking to curtail demographic growth in predominantly Black wards in the city.

The Hooks Brothers were there from the beginning to document "Bob" Church's evolution as one of the most significant African American politicians of the early twentieth century. An early example is a widely circulated portrait created during the 1910s, (**Fig. 2**).[17] This image first circulated in a number of African American newspapers at the time, and was also published in books on African American history by Black authors, such as Thomas O. Fuller's *Pictorial History of the American Negro (1933)*.[18] It is a bust-length photograph, wherein Church sits facing the viewer, but his head is angled toward the light source. Turning the head allows the photographer to profile his face against a dark background, emphasizing the subject's light-colored skin. Church's tailored tweed jacket and vest fit to perfection. As observed in almost every photograph taken of Robert Church, he is seldom without the immaculate white handkerchief appropriately placed in his left breast pocket. The style of portraiture is reminiscent of Victorian era, late nineteenth-century portrait traditions that borrowed from European aristocratic painting in order to elevate photography to the level of fine art.

According to Alan Trachtenberg in *Reading American Photographs*, the goal of photographic portraits imitating portrait painting was to capture the "soul of the subject itself."[19] The photographer should not aim to represent nature simply as it is, but to create an ideal type. Successful portraits, therefore, revealed what could not be seen, such as the inner essence of the subject, the expression of character, intelligence, vision, and discipline. Much of the effort to visually express unseen qualities like cultural refinement and fineness of character centered upon the eyes and the position of the head. By the 1850s professional photographers advised

Fig. 2. Robert R. Church Jr., 1910s
Hooks Brothers. Church Family Papers,
Special Collections-University of Memphis

the sitter to avert the eyes and gaze off into the distance as seen here. Victorian era sensibilities considered looking directly at the viewer as if the subject was conscious of the audience and the process of portrait making ill-mannered and lowly.

These formal conventions of portrait photography were adapted to the African American subject as well. In *Photography on the Color Line: W. E. B. Du Bois, Race, and Visual Culture,* Shawn Michelle Smith argues that the larger format of cabinet cards, such this example, encouraged bust poses and a focus on the individual's face and expression.[20] Portraits of African American male subjects also tended to be closely cropped, so that the shoulders and head filled the frame. While the features were strongly lighted, ample space was maintained around the head. Squarely centered, the African American male subject was also advised to stare past the viewer, fixing his gaze on something outside the picture's frame of reference. Hence, the turned head and averted gaze in the Church portrait effectively conveys a semblance of refinement and class distinction appropriate to the subject and his exalted position of leadership in Memphis. It is a representation of a certain type of African American manhood that promises achievement on the national stage as well. The Hooks Brothers and Robert Church Jr. therefore collaborated to create a model of racial representation that largely conformed to the "New Negro" aesthetic.[21] The self-representation of Robert Church Jr., like the photographs in Dubois' American Negro Exhibit, adheres to the ideology that it is the middle-class elite, or what Du Bois termed "the talented tenth"' that should determine the standard and lead the way in African American progress.

REPRESENTING BLACK BUSINESS SUCCESS

An important example of Robert and Henry's visual documentation of Black businesses in Memphis is the photograph, *New Era Pharmacy*, 1915, **(Fig.3)**.[22] Located at 327 Beale Street, the drugstore was established by George R. Jackson, a graduate of the pharmacy school at the University of Michigan. The use of large eight- by ten-inch glass plates allowed the Hooks Brothers to incorporate extensive visual details, including a diversity of objects and texts, in spite of the store's long, rather dark, recessed space. Light reflecting off the mirrors on the back wall, rear table, glass cabinets and jars, as well as the vertical soda fountain on the opposite counter, help to widen the room's narrow confines. The lighting effects encourage the viewer to look intently, enhancing visual points of interest and reflection.

The *New Era Pharmacy* was a typical early twentieth-century drugstore, well stocked with prescription drugs and medicines, (carefully compounded according to advertisements), toilet articles, cigars, candies, perfumes, brushes, and cosmetics. It boasted a fine soda fountain, and accommodated visitors and customers with small elegant tables and chairs for seating. Magazines and newspapers provided reading material and encourage customers to linger. Additional graphic materials, like posters, signs, calendars, and diplomas, highlighted the attractiveness of the space as a social gathering place.

The poster attached to the side of the cabinet advertised a concert by the Williams Family, "world famous colored singers." Stacked above it in a pyramid shape were small containers featuring George Washington's face as part of the graphic design. A sign next to the university diploma encouraged Blacks to save for the holidays by investing in a Christmas Fund sponsored by the Solvent Savings Bank. Established by Robert R. Church Sr., it was the first Black bank in Memphis, providing critical economic support for many of the Black businesses that flourished around Beale Street during the turn of the century. The large sign near the ceiling proclaimed that the Memphis Colored Fair, to take place on October, 11th, 12th, and 13th, would be bigger and better than ever.

Even the name Dr. Jackson chose for his pharmacy signifies the New Negro philosophy of social uplift, and the leadership role Dubois assigned to the African American professional elite, the well-educated, and the successful entrepreneur. The overcrowded shelves in the handsome wood cabinets skillfully highlighted by the Hooks Brothers' camerawork revealed that Dr. Jackson could afford to fully stock his pharmacy with medicines and health-related items he was professionally trained to administer. African Americans in the city may have had difficulty accessing the necessary medicinal items anywhere else except in a Black- owned pharmacy. Beyond that, this modern public space is portrayed as a stylish gathering place for young and old alike, where African Americans could get prescriptions filled, drink sodas, read the latest magazines, and get information about current events.

Fig.3. New Era Pharmacy, 1915.
Hooks Brothers. Department of Art-University of Memphis

BLACK PATRIOTISM IN WORLD WAR I

African American soldiers' experiences abroad during the Great War were a significant stimulus to the "New Negro" movement. They were exposed to a freedom of mobility denied them back home. By the end of World War I, over three hundred and fifty thousand Black men had served in the American Expeditionary Forces on the Western Front. Some forty thousand men from Shelby County were drafted or served as volunteers. Upon their return, Black men were increasingly impatient with racial discrimination. The result was the eruption of race riots across the country in the summer of 1919.

Hooks Brothers' photographs documented the African American involvement in the Great War. They are particularly strong in the representation of Black women and their efforts to participate in the Great War as professional nurses, despite constantly encountering racist roadblocks. The American Red Cross established a presence in the Mid-South when it opened a branch during the war in 1917 as the Memphis-Shelby County Chapter serving the Tri-State area. An auxiliary "colored" counterpart was founded, known as the "Solvent Branch Red Cross Headquarters, Memphis Tennessee." The Solvent Branch was located in the Solvent Savings Bank, the first Black bank founded by Robert Church Sr. in 1909. The setting for two extant photographs picturing the auxiliary branch were taken in the financial institution's Beale Street location, highlighting the proactive role local Black institutions played in the war effort.[23] The bank location became the center of war-related activities in the Black community, including Liberty Bond and war saving stamp initiatives, as well as the segregated branch of the Red Cross.

The Hooks Brothers' photographs of this establishment are valuable records of the expression of patriotism in Memphis' African American community during the Great War. They are well-lit, well-composed, sharply-focused images representative of the high technical skill level of the photographers. One of the two extant photographs shows Black nurses proudly outfitted in the traditional uniforms of Red Cross nurses (**Fig.4**). They are working in a long narrow room that obviously functioned as a sewing operation. At least seven sewing machines were made available for women to work on, while others stitched materials by hand. Posters of different sizes decorate the walls. The eye is drawn to the back of the room,

Headquarters "Solvent Branch" Red Cross
Headquarters, Memphis, Tennessee.
They Made many thousands of articles
for our boys in France.

Fig.4. Red Cross Branch-Solvent Savings Bank location, 1918. Hooks Brothers.
Miles Vandahurst Lynk, The Negro Pictorial Review of the Great World War;
a Visual Narrative of the Negro's Glorious Part in the World's Greatest War
(Memphis), Twentieth Century Art Company,(c.1919), p.36.

Fig.5. Red Cross Branch-Solvent Savings Bank location, 1918.

Hooks Brothers. Pink Palace Museum collection

Fig. 6. Nurses, Jane Terrell Hospital, 1910s.

Hooks Brothers. Department of Art-University of Memphis

where two men stand next to a large poster; the imagery is blurred, but it is likely related to supporting the war effort, similar to the large vertical poster with the Red Cross symbol on the left wall.[24]

The other photograph is set in a different room of the Solvent Savings Bank building. It is a wide, more shallow room that looks like it served as the canteen, or social gathering place-eatery for the soldiers (Fig.5). American flags and flags of some of the allies, as well as posters decorate the walls. Eleven Red Cross nurses mingle with twelve men in uniform. The eye is drawn to the center of the room where five soldiers sit at the table. Other than the seated soldier drinking a Coke, the type of food that predominates is fruit. This indicates that the organization encouraged conventional activities that supported the war, such as promoting nutritional foodstuffs and habits of consumption. The image likewise exhibits some of the sewn handiwork of the women, such as the quilt and white pillow with the Red Cross symbol placed on the sofa extending from the right of the picture frame.

The two photographs highlight the significant history of early Black medical training in Memphis. The Black nurses pictured in the two images would have likely graduated from one of three training schools in the city. In 1909, two small hospitals serving the African American community in Memphis merged to establish the Jane Terrell Hospital located at 698 Williams Avenue. It had two operating rooms, one hundred beds, and a training school for nurses, making it the first hospital to graduate Black nurses in Memphis (Fig.6).[25] The women might have been graduates of the nursing program at the University of West Tennessee, founded in Jackson, Tennessee, by Dr. Miles Vandahurst Lynk in 1900 and relocated to Memphis in 1908. Educating African Americans in the medical professions (including physicians, pharmacists, dentists, and nurses), the institution trained most of the city's early doctors and dentists during its twenty-three years of existence.[26] Collins Chapel Hospital launched in 1910 during the era of Jim Crow to provide healthcare for Blacks in segregated Memphis. It was especially proud of the "Training School for Nurses" established in connection with the hospital.[27]

These educational sources for training Black nurses in Memphis, as well as the support of Black economic institutions like the Solvent Savings Bank, likely factored into the decision to locate an auxiliary branch of the Red Cross in the city's African American community. The Hooks Brothers' visual recordings of these events provide specific documentation of patriotic activity in Memphis. They captured Black southern women's attitudes towards the Great War as well as the manner in which the government sought to control and regulate their incorporation into the war effort. Although forced to work within segregated spaces, the Hooks Brothers artistry, as seen in the formally-organized and technically-skilled representation of the Black nurses, transmits beyond the confines of the two rooms in which they are pictured or the limitations of racism. The Hooks Brother succeeded in conveying something of the nature of Black women's patriotism, expressed in the fact of their professional training and the understanding of how patriotic work could be used to improve the social conditions of the Black community.[28]

CONCLUSION

The Hooks Brothers were exceptional photographers. They have left behind a body of work that documents the first eighty years of the twentieth century in the urban South. Specifically, the work deals with at least four generations of the middle-class community in Memphis. I have culled from their vast oeuvre a few seminal photographs that exemplify the cultural expression and ideology known as the "New Negro movement." The early Hooks Brothers' photographs parallel the artistry of James Van Der Zee in Harlem and Addison Scurlock in Washington, DC. These early African American photographers collaborated with their subjects in the creation of a certain type of visual representation that worked against the White racist imaging of Blackness pervasive in early twentieth century American popular culture.[29] The Hooks Brothers were an important part of this movement in the urban South, participating in the politics of cultural representation and its relationship to the early civil rights struggle during the first decades of the twentieth century.

CHAPTER TWELVE

MEMPHIS BURNING

Preston Lauterbach

In the afternoon of February 26, 1953, fire destroyed a landmark in south Memphis, on Lauderdale Street. A stately three-story home, with eighteen rooms and twin gables, burned from its spires down.

Firefighters weren't late to the blaze — in fact, they'd ignited it. The city of Memphis, which was then hosting a convention of fire safety officials from around the country, had authorized the burning of the vacant mansion in order to demonstrate a new, efficient, fog nozzle fire-hose. Thousands stood in the street to watch. For two hours, firemen in black helmets and black slickers fought flames that burst through the roof and out of the windows. After blasting down each fire, they set another part of the home ablaze. Afterwards, the ruins steamed.

But there was much more to this demonstration than a test of new firefighting equipment. As locals understood, the burning of this particular home was an assertion of power, because of who it had belonged to and what it symbolized. Abandoned, weather-beaten, but still grand, the mansion at 384 South Lauderdale represented the pinnacle of black achievement in the city.

THE FIRE

A man named Robert Reed Church had built that home seventy years earlier. Church, though born a slave, made a fortune in real estate and was known as the South's first black millionaire. He helped lead the rebuilding of Memphis after yellow fever nearly wiped out the city in the 1870s, and from there he became the key developer of an iconic thoroughfare, presiding over a thriving African-American community on Beale Street. The street is legendary as the home of the blues, but it also nurtured early civil rights activism, notably in the work of crusading journalist Ida B. Wells, and black political power, through Robert Church's son, known in civic circles nationwide as Bob Church.

Bob was born and grew up in the fine house on Lauderdale Street, a half mile from a city park named for his father, in circumstances quite unlike what most African Americans knew. Not only had he come into the world in a mansion, all he could see out its windows were houses like his. Inside those houses lived prosperous whites — the families of U.S. Senator Kenneth McKellar and Supreme Court Justice Abe Fortas — and successful blacks, like city councilman Lymus Wallace and Julia and Charles Hooks, a music teacher and juvenile court judge, respectively, whose grandson Benjamin went on to lead the NAACP.

When Bob was born, in 1885, ten black families lived among whites on three blocks of South Lauderdale. In 1900, there were eleven black households; in 1910, there were ten. The decennial census is a small sample, but it shows a stable, racially mixed neighborhood in the heart of the South, during what were bleak decades for African Americans. And these weren't Negro servants living in backhouse quarters, but a professional class of homeowners. A child growing up on this street would have absorbed a certain sense of equality. These white families tolerated black neighbors, and these black families kept pace with white elites. According to racist doctrine in the post-Reconstruction South, nothing about this was normal.

Robert Church, Sr., groomed his son as his heir in business. He founded a bank and put Bob in charge; built an auditorium and put Bob in charge; and consolidated his real estate holdings, including modest but attractive homes for African-American renters, into the R.R. Church & Son company, making Bob president. But the son yearned for politics. Determined to fight for racial equality, Bob Church saw the greatest opportunity to make a difference at the ballot box.

As a rising Republican star in the early 20th century — at that time the G.O.P. was still the party of Lincoln, and therefore had virtually the entire black vote — the younger Church achieved tremendous victories. He organized and registered black voters, and in 1920 helped win Tennessee for Warren Harding, the first time since 1876 that a former Confederate state had gone Republican in a presidential election. As the chief patronage dispenser in Memphis, Church controlled numerous federally appointed jobs, from postal workers to district attorneys. An admiring foe noted that he had a hotline running from Beale Street to the White House. Memphis blacks revered Church and all he stood for. The house on South Lauderdale symbolized his family's courage, drive, and success, and demonstrated the potential of black power in Memphis. Bob Church strove to make black people "politically active," in his words.

Meanwhile, a new power was rising in the form of a political machine controlled by Edward Hull "Boss" Crump. The white Democrat had moved to Memphis from Holly Springs, Mississippi, the same town where Robert Church, Sr., was born. Crump was elected mayor in 1909, at age thirty-five, and resigned in 1916. From then until his death in 1954, he ran Memphis as the undisputed boss of a formidable political machine. With his clouds of white hair, bushy eyebrows, and flashy attire, Crump cut an iconic figure, and his sharp wit made him good copy for *Time* and the *Saturday Evening Post*. He characterized one opponent as "the kind of man who'd milk his neighbor's cow through the fence."

On the surface, Bob Church and Boss Crump, the black Republican and white Democrat, would seem to be natural enemies, yet for a time the two men coexisted and even partnered. In the 1920s, they led a bipartisan, biracial coalition that controlled Memphis politics and elected most of its officials. Crump encouraged the black vote, and in return Church used his sway with Republican presidents to help place friendly officials in federal posts, while protecting the Crump machine from federal investigation. Together, they helmed Memphis through a time of exceptional growth, until the Great Depression hit.

This period of biracial cooperation was short-lived. In the late 1930s, Boss Crump turned on Church. In the span of a few years, the Democratic machine banished Church, seized his property, broke the family fortune, and dismantled his Republican organization, crushing the most vital arm of black enfranchisement in the city.

The betrayal was mostly a matter of political expediency. With Franklin Roosevelt in the Oval Office, Crump no longer needed a Republican ally. As one of his operatives explained, "Pendergast, Daley, Roosevelt, Crump, the one characteristic that they all had in common was the ability, when necessary, to be absolutely and completely ruthless when it came to the organization. ... I don't care how close a person was to them, how loyal they'd been, how much they had accomplished, as soon as they felt like they were no longer politically advantageous, out they went." But even by that callous standard, the excommunication of Bob Church was particularly vicious. Crump accused Church of spreading dangerous ideas, and he told the editor of the black *Memphis World*, "You have a bunch of niggers teaching social equality, stirring up racial hatred. I am not going to stand for it. I've dealt with niggers all my life, and I know how to treat them. ... This is Memphis."

Smoke in the Memphis sky on that day in February 1953 signaled Crump's complete triumph, as the former Church mansion was burned to the ground. "An act of infamy," the black *Tri-State Defender* called it. Decades later, a black Memphis resident, Lester Lynom, described it as "almost a lynching of the Negroes of Memphis." He added, "It wasn't just the house, it was what the house represented."

THE BULLDOZERS

When Crump turned on Church in the 1930s, the machine initiated the federally funded "slum clearance" of ten blocks across the street from the Church family home. The clearance area, west of Lauderdale from Vance Avenue to Mississippi Boulevard, featured houses that ranged in size from the Church mansion to the Hooks' single-story, single-family home, and small businesses such as flower shops, groceries, cafes, and funeral parlors. The structures were no more than sixty years old, and the few surviving dwellings from that era attest to their sturdy construction.

Residents beseeched Senator McKellar, their onetime neighbor and a conduit of federal authority, not to "wreck this whole section of the city," as one letter put it. "The home owners are sick and distressed beyond measure." They wrote that that they had toiled for years to pay off their mortgages and fix up their properties, and they'd succeeded in making this the best neighborhood for blacks in Memphis. Their community was more valuable than any relocation funds the city might provide. One of Crump's leading black organizers, the Reverend T.O. Fuller, protested that he'd lose his home, workplace, and church.

Their grievances were ignored. The Memphis Housing Authority — established in the mid-'30s under Roosevelt's New Deal — leveled a 46-acre area and replaced the single-family homes with a low-rise, 900-unit public housing complex. As justification, the Housing Authority cited statistics showing that the city's black population had doubled in less than thirty years. Densifying an existing black neighborhood was a racist strategy to prevent African Americans from encroaching on predominantly white areas. The complex, known as William H. Foote Homes, opened in 1940 — directly across the street from the Robert Church house.

What was left of the city's most prosperous, integrated neighborhood began to deteriorate. Surrounded by dense, low-income housing, the fine Victorian homes were subdivided and turned into cheap rooming houses. The city — which had previously allowed Bob Church to skip paying property taxes — foreclosed on his estate and auctioned off ten properties to pay the tax debt.

Two decades later, the Crump machine finished the job. Another slum clearance program demolished the area east of Lauderdale, including the vacant lot where the Church mansion had stood, and in 1955 the MHA opened the 650-unit Edward O. Cleaborn Homes. Both public housing complexes were designated exclusively for African Americans.

Thus Boss Crump converted one of the black community's greatest strengths into a monument to inequality. No one had ever studied the neighborhood to figure out how it worked, how it had thrived for a half century when social equality failed nearly everywhere else in Memphis, and nearly everywhere throughout the South. Instead, federal funds enabled one group to hold down another, as Boss Crump crushed Bob Church's movement for black political power.

THE BOMB

Inequality is *enforced* in Memphis, and it always has been. The city was founded on the backs of slaves, as the capital of a cotton empire that stretched across the Mississippi Delta. The great river connected the city to the slave port at New Orleans, while a railroad linked Memphis to another slave port at Charleston, South Carolina. Confederate icon Nathan Bedford Forrest, both a slave trader and an alderman, helped shape the city's identity, investing in the Memphis-Charleston railroad and pushing local ordinances to benefit the business of slavery. Emancipation did little to change his outlook on labor conditions. When asked in 1869 who could solve the shortage of farm workers in west Tennessee, Forrest responded, "Get them from Africa. If you put them in squads of ten, with one experienced leader in each squad, they will soon revive our country." He had already imported one such lot for his Mississippi plantation, boasting, "They were very fond of grasshoppers and bugs, and I taught them to eat cooked meat, and they were as good niggers as I ever had."

Cotton continued to dominate the Memphis economy after the Civil War, with black hands to do the planting, weeding, picking, baling, and the hauling to brokerages and warehouses along the river. Even as the industry declined, the crop defined the city's identity. The annual Cotton Carnival celebrated a "King" and "Queen" who were drawn ceremonially through the streets in a parade of floats carried by shirtless black men in frayed knickers.

In 1953, the year of the burning of the old Church home, the Memphis Urban League reported that the median income for black households was $1,348 annually, less than half the white median of $3,085. These figures represent Memphis inequality in the last years of the Crump era. Roughly 23,000 black families lived in extreme poverty, making less than $1,000 annually, and more black families were grouped in the sub-$500 category than in any other bracket. "Can anyone be amazed when these people appear in large numbers on relief rolls, in juvenile and criminal courts, and as contributors to illegitimacy, delinquency?" observed an official of the Urban League. "Their plight is the result of cheap labor, poor schools, and slums." Inequality was also firmly established at the upper end of the scale. Of the 4,000 Memphis families earning $10,000 or more annually, only 35 were black.

Crump is the master behind the city's narrative, and his legacy lives on. His rule was so absolute, following his destruction of the black Republican organization, that the boss faced no real opposition. He handpicked local officials and candidates who did things the Crump way. According to former machine operative Guy Bates, Crump's reign did lasting damage to the city's long-term development. When the boss died in 1954 he left no heir, and his style of governing allowed no room for competing visions or compromise. No one was ready to take over. "We had generations of office holders and people that literally couldn't think for themselves. He stifled all other political thoughts," Bates said. "Where Houston grew, Dallas grew, and Atlanta grew, Memphis stayed where Mr. Crump wanted it to stay."

Today, the majority-black city ranks high nationally in both overall and child poverty, among large metro areas. A recent study found that 68 percent of the population lives in economic distress, as measured by indices of educational attainment, unemployment, median income, vacant houses, and shuttered businesses. And nearly 80 percent of the poor are black. Elena Delavega at the University of Memphis has reported that black poverty in the city ranks far above state and national averages, while poverty among non-Hispanic whites is below average. Memphis also ranks near the top for murders, aggravated assaults, and robberies per capita.

Of course, poverty and crime are the symptoms of inequality, not its root causes. To truly understand racial inequality in America, you have to start with housing. In Memphis, inequality between black and white citizens is enforced at the neighborhood level, block by block, house by house.

The burning of the Church family home was far from the last fire in the housing battle. Four months later, on June 28, 1953, an explosion shattered windows at a house two miles away, sending residents of the block running for cover. Integration of that neighborhood had begun peacefully enough — years, in fact, before the integration of city schools, before the desegregation of public washrooms and dining rooms, and before downtown department stores and cafeterias served white and black customers equally. South Memphis could have been the model for an integrated Memphis. The bomb changed all that.

The house that exploded, at 430 East Olive Avenue, had been recently sold to the Williams family, the sixth or seventh black household to move into a neighborhood of small cottages occupied mainly by whites. Apparently, that was one black family too many. Soon after they moved in, white neighbors formed a violent, reactionary mob, shouting epithets at the new residents, patrolling the streets and taking down *For Sale* signs. They threatened to tar and feather homeowners who sold to black buyers. "When they see a house being shown, they round up the mob," said Mrs. L.C. Hauser, a white resident of East Olive. "It's like the Paul Revere signal."

The explosion ignited citywide discussion of "the housing problem," as a rapidly growing black population challenged the status quo of racially segregated neighborhoods. African-American leader Benjamin Hooks — the future NAACP director and FCC commissioner who had grown up on Lauderdale near the Church family — wrote to the mayor: "There is an urgent demand for additional housing facilities for Negroes, which can only be met by natural area expansion ... the extension of Negro home ownership into ever-widening areas." This was a clear warning that the clash on Olive Avenue would be repeated, as black families continued their movement into formerly all-white neighborhoods.

Two months after the bombing, a group of white Olive Avenue residents called on the mayor. They planned to sell their houses, and they wanted the city's protection from the mob. "Mr. Mayor, these Negroes who have moved in there seem to be a fine class of Negroes," remarked one. "They keep up their homes and they look better than when the white people owned them." The group assured the mayor that they didn't object to the presence of blacks: "We object to the whites." But in any case, they were getting out. One owner reported, "My husband says he'll move and let that house sit there empty before he'll stay there. We do not want our children in that situation." Another neatly summarized the theme of the next five decades of Memphis history, telling the mayor, "You have to get out of that neighborhood if you want decent children."

These events took place a year before the U.S. Supreme Court overturned the "separate but equal" doctrine and a year before the death of Boss Crump. But between Brown v. Board and Mr. Edward Hull Crump, it was no contest: the boss would have a much longer afterlife in the city of Memphis.

Today, East Olive Avenue looks as though more than one stick of dynamite went off. Where neat, solid frame houses once stood on tidy little lawns, now derelict buildings are collapsing between overgrown vacant lots. It exemplifies the cycle of fight, flight, and blight that has made Memphis what it is today.

THE GUNSHOT

Fifteen years after the bombing of the house on East Olive, the city's reputation for inequality was reinforced by one of history's greatest tragedies.

In early 1968, city sanitation workers went on strike, appealing for higher wages, better working conditions, and union recognition, following the deaths of two workers who were crushed in a garbage truck. Memphis was now ruled by Mayor Henry Loeb — a staunch segregationist and true successor to Crump. Loeb refused their demands, and the confrontation quickly became not just a labor dispute but a matter of civil rights, attracting national leaders like NAACP head Roy Wilkins and Dr. Martin Luther King, Jr.

King made three trips to Memphis during the strike, first to speak at a rally on March 18, then to lead a demonstration that exploded into a riot on March 28. The riot hurt King's reputation for nonviolence, and his associates organized another event, "the makeup march," to prove that a peaceful demonstration could be held in Memphis. King returned to the city on April 3, and that evening delivered one of his most famous speeches, "I've Been to the Mountaintop":

Like anybody, I would like to live a long life. Longevity has its place. But I'm not concerned about that now. I just want to do God's will. And He's allowed me to go up to the mountain. And I've looked over. And I've seen the Promised Land. I may not get there with you. But I want you to know tonight, that we, as a people, will get to the promised land! And so I'm happy, tonight. I'm not worried about anything. I'm not fearing any man! Mine eyes have seen the glory of the coming of the Lord!

The next evening, King was fatally shot on the balcony of the Lorraine Motel in downtown Memphis. The assassination stands out not only as a signal moment in American history, but also as a powerful example of the consequences of bad leadership. For in Memphis the persistence of inequality is inextricably bound up with the city's long decline, and Loeb's obstinance seems as crucial to its social psychology as Boss Crump's bulldozers were to its built environment.

Historian Kenneth T. Jackson of Columbia University is a preeminent scholar of suburbanization and author of *The Crabgrass Frontier*. He's also a Memphian, born and raised during the Crump reign. "Seventy years ago, Memphis, Atlanta, and Dallas were more or less in the same place, size-wise," he said. Memphis had the advantage of the Mississippi River as well as rail and interstate highway connections; its economy should have kept pace with, if not surpassed, its southern peers. Instead, Jackson said, it "got obliterated by those other cities."

While Atlanta leadership embraced a racially progressive, pro-business attitude behind Mayor Ivan Allen — adopting the slogan, *The City Too Busy to Hate* — Memphis "got on the wrong side of the civil rights revolution," Jackson said. "I would put a lot of the blame on Henry Loeb." He recalled watching the TV news the day of King's funeral in Atlanta, and seeing the mayor of that city hold an umbrella for Coretta Scott King. "Same night, same news, Henry Loeb was apoplectic, talking about how outside agitators had caused all of this," Jackson said. As the nation mourned, white leaders in Memphis were tragically out of step. *Time* called Memphis a "decaying Mississippi river town," blaming the assassination on "intransigent white mayor Henry Loeb" and his refusal to meet "modest wage and compensation demands."

To this day, many believe that King's death coincided with the death of Memphis, that it marked the beginning of a half century of decline. It's a convenient notion, but it doesn't ring true. The assassination merely punctuated events set in motion decades earlier, when Boss Crump suppressed Bob Church's dream of social equality and economic justice.

THE RETREAT

White flight intensified the geography of disparity. Beginning in the 1950s, working-class whites moved just beyond the city's boundaries, first north to Frayser and south to Whitehaven, and then "out East" to Germantown, Collierville, and Cordova, where they built roads, schools, shopping centers, and hospitals — all the features of a city, spread over small rural communities. The completion of the I-240 freeway loop, in 1984, directed commerce away from the urban core of Memphis and toward the suburbs. Today, the highest concentrations of wealth, educational attainment, and jobs are on the eastern edge.

In an ongoing effort to recapture its lost revenue base, Memphis has annexed this ever-expanding crabgrass frontier so that it can collect property taxes from white flighters. Over time, the city has grown to a sprawling 324 square miles, larger than New York City, Atlanta, or St. Louis, without increasing its population of 650,000. Now the city government is responsible for providing services to that vast area, and yet the county roll shows that a third of the land — 95 square miles — is essentially vacant, and much more is sparsely populated. In several cases the city gambled badly, annexing planned developments that never materialized, and now its diminished resources are spread thin across an ever larger territory, much of which generates no revenue.

In modern Memphis there is no figurehead, no Henry Loeb or Boss Crump, to articulate and symbolize the tenets of white supremacy. In fact, one result of white flight and black population growth has been the ascent of African-American political leadership. In 1974, Harold Ford, Sr., won election to the U.S. House of Representatives, becoming the state's first black congressman. In 1991, former school superintendent Dr. Willie Herenton became the city's first African-American mayor. But the election of black leaders has done nothing to end racial division in Memphis — today, white opposition is expressed in continual growth beyond the city. In suburban malls and parks, you hear the loud echo of those nice white ladies in the mayor's office in 1953: "You have to get out of that neighborhood if you want decent children."

The racial prejudice of many suburbanites is revealed by their hostility to integrated public schools. Over the years, proposals to merge the government of surrounding Shelby County with the city government never gained much traction — but when county and city *schools* were finally merged, in 2011, that sparked a new segregationist revolt. Within two years, six suburban municipalities withdrew from the consolidated system and established their own schools (with a huge assist from the state legislature, which changed a law that had prohibited new school districts), and now those suburban districts no longer need to share their resources with the city. Urban residents nonetheless pay both city and county property taxes, benefiting the communities that have withdrawn their resources from Memphis.

The U.S. Census Bureau's 2011 American Community Survey shows the magnitude of disparity between Memphis proper and its suburbs out East. The wealthiest, best-educated households live clustered among the best job opportunities east of the city, while the least educated, most impoverished households live near low-skill, low-wage jobs. The survey found the city's unemployment rate to be double the national average, with black unemployment double that of whites. Median annual household income in Memphis proper was $37,072, compared with $46,102 in Shelby County (including the city) and $51,324 nationally.

THE MONEY

The closest thing modern Memphis has to an era-defining figure is Robert Lipscomb. Quite unlike the audacious Boss Crump, Lipscomb is soft-spoken and nonpolitical. He is also African American, a graduate of storied Booker T. Washington High School in South Memphis. As head of Housing and Community Development from 1992 to 2015, he led many of the signature initiatives of Mayor Herenton and oversaw the transformation of public housing. For a time, he held three high-ranking posts simultaneously, as head of HCD, director of the Memphis Housing Authority, and chief financial officer of the city. That made him the municipal leader most directly engaged with poverty in Memphis.

Lipscomb is like Crump in one crucial respect: for many years his actual power transcended his official authority. He outlasted the five-term mayor who appointed him and continued to play a central role in public policy — perhaps *the* central role — through the next two mayoral terms. In late 2015, he was ousted from power amid allegations of sexual abuse. Yet his legacy will shape Memphis for generations. He had such a profound influence on the built environment that he's compared to Robert Moses, the powerful midcentury planner of New York City. With that comparison comes the insinuation — sometimes the open accusation — that he wielded too much power.

Certainly his power is evident in the transformation of public housing that's happened in the past quarter century. When Lipscomb joined the Herenton administration, there were six public housing projects in Memphis. When Lipscomb left office, only Foote Homes remained. The rest had been redeveloped under HOPE VI, a Clinton-era initiative that replaces rundown public housing with new, mixed-income developments and turns them over to private management. Lipscomb leveraged tens of millions of federal dollars to demolish the old projects and then partnered with commercial developers to build new affordable housing.

The contrast can be seen clearly on Lauderdale Street, near the former site of the Church family home. On the west side of the street, the squat, brick buildings of Foote Homes glower behind a high black fence. On the east side, the Cleaborn Homes have been torn down and replaced by "Cleaborn Pointe at Heritage Landing," a HOPE VI development of clean pastel townhouses with bright white trim. Likewise, in North Memphis, the Housing Authority under Lipscomb demolished the notorious Hurt Village projects and created the 100-block Uptown redevelopment area, where young professionals live among lower-income residents whose housing is subsidized by federal Section 8 vouchers.

Critics say such efforts don't cure poverty so much as they improve neighborhood appearances and line the pockets of private developers. Steve Lockwood, who runs a community development corporation in Frayser, just north of Uptown, said that his neighborhood now has the highest concentration of Section 8 residents in the city. He associates rising violent crime with an influx of people displaced from Hurt Village.

Housing is not the only sphere in which Lipscomb wielded outsized power. People need jobs as well as shelter, and as it turns out, those pretty pastel redevelopments are located far from the city's best opportunities. Wearing his other hat, as HCD director, Lipscomb was charged with stimulating economic growth in the urban core. Here his legacy is especially controversial. Whereas Housing Boss Lipscomb administered the flow of federal dollars tied to specific projects, Development Boss Lipscomb controlled discretionary funds in the form of Community Development Block Grants. Both funding streams are administered by the federal department of Housing and Urban Development, but the CDBGs come with far fewer restrictions. Which meant that in practice, one man — Robert Lipscomb — could use the community development grants however he liked, within the broad mandate of creating economic growth in impoverished areas. Almost any project could be justified.

With significant federal funds at his discretion, Lipscomb was the point man between the city government and the nonprofit CDCs that operate at a neighborhood scale — and that all across Memphis struggle with the fallout of white flight, with surging crime, failing schools, and blighted properties. The CDCs have scant resources. In contrast, the federal dollars flowing through Housing and Community Development represent the largest pot of money this poverty-stricken city has ever had for alleviating social problems. No private charity or public entity came close to Lipscomb's budget.

Of the dozen or so sources interviewed for this story, all people who are deeply engaged with poverty and inequality in Memphis, none hesitated to bring up Lipscomb by name or to question how "the city" — synonymous with Lipscomb — spends its resources. Two concerns were raised by nearly everyone. First is the disparity between the meager funds spent at the neighborhood level, on CDC programs that assist small businesses and finance home repairs and construction in blighted areas, and the much larger sums of money funneled into big business projects, including for-profit ventures. The second is how the misuse of those federal millions reveals a lack of comprehensive planning.

Attorneys Webb Brewer and Steve Barlow have been engaged in fair housing suits in Memphis for two decades, and in that time they have worked both for and against the city government. In one recent, high-profile case, they represented the city in a predatory lending lawsuit against Wells-Fargo that resulted in a $7.5 million settlement. In fact, it was Lipscomb who alerted Brewer and Barlow to an unusually high number of foreclosures against black homeowners in economically depressed areas.

Despite their professional connections to the city, the attorneys are sharply critical of how funds have been distributed. "If you look at what they were spent for, it's all on macroeconomic development deals," Barlow said. His partner explained how the city has done an end run around federal guidelines that specify that funds must benefit low- and moderate-income people. "What they've gotten away with here forever is saying, 'This is going to provide jobs,'" Brewer said. He cited the widening of Poplar Avenue, the main artery leading out East, as a project funded with community development grants that actually benefited "business people" above all.

Federal money also helped build a new downtown basketball arena and, later, convert the old arena, The Pyramid, into a sporting goods megastore. The Pyramid project was locally notorious: it dragged on for nearly ten years, which did as much to inflame anti-Lipscomb sentiment as the millions of public dollars committed to the conversion of a civic venue (owned and operated by the city of Memphis and Shelby County) into a private business. The Pyramid finally reopened as a Bass Pro Shop that includes a hotel, restaurant, and observation deck overlooking the Mississippi River. As with other projects, the city justified its allocation of HUD funds by promising to create jobs, and federal administrators accepted that at face value.

Yet no matter such promises, it's clear that inequality and poverty haven't statistically improved, despite decades of investment. One specific case seems particularly wasteful: the city's investment in the Peabody Place project, located not a mile from the old Church family home. In 1998, Lipscomb's division gave $1.2 million to Belz Enterprises, the developer of Peabody Place and the nearby Gibson Guitar Factory — the first installment in what would become a steady stream of federal funds that passed through the city to the project. Peabody Place mall opened in 2001, featuring tenants like Gap, Starbucks, and a twenty-screen movieplex; by 2012 it had closed, a casualty of the Great Recession. Over a decade and a half, the city provided more than $26 million in assistance, including $2.7 million in Community Development Block Grants, $14.9 million from a HUD Urban Development Action Grant, and $9.9 million in the form of a Section 108 loan. All those millions amounted to zero long-term job growth, and community activists believe the funds should have gone instead toward tangible improvement at the neighborhood level.

Tom Burns is an urban planning consultant who came to Memphis to work with a local nonprofit focused on neighborhood revitalization. He's been in the field for forty years and has consulted in cities — including

Detroit and Baltimore — that also struggle with poverty, blight, and a lack of resources. In Memphis, he interviewed the heads of some twenty HUD-approved community development corporations. It turns out, "they're not getting a lot of city money," Burns said. "Why, given the evident patterns of inequity, [is] there ... so little attention and investment in government toward neighborhood revitalization?"

Burns was impressed by Lipscomb's housing achievements, particularly the HOPE VI development in Cleaborn Pointe. And yet, he said, other projects showed that city planners were making no connection between multimillion-dollar municipal investments and the neighborhoods that urgently needed help. "The scale of the problems here is enormous," he said, "but if you're trying to make a big difference, you have to link things up in a way that builds momentum. I don't see the civic leaders connecting the dots." *Connecting the dots*, he said, means linking housing developments to centers of job growth. It means avoiding public-private projects that lack a direct connection to neighborhood concerns. It means avoiding The Pyramid.

The city may no longer have a boss, but nearly a century after it was founded, the Memphis machine is alive and kicking. Here, in the nation's poorest major city, powerful local developers and corporations are siphoning off federal anti-poverty subsidies that should go directly to stimulate the economic progress of poor neighborhoods. That's pretty much the definition of inequality. Boss Lipscomb will be remembered for tearing down the neglected housing projects that symbolized the overt racism of earlier leaders, but he will also be remembered for controlling the purse-strings of a city government that provided a wealthy elite with resources that the poor majority desperately needed.

THE FUTURE

Although Robert Lipscomb had seemed invincible for a generation, his critics now get to see how the city works without its powerbroker.

Lipscomb's reign ended with a late-night announcement that the HCD director had stepped down following a criminal complaint that he had engaged in sexual relations with a minor. When reporters rang the bell the next morning, he answered his front door wearing an undershirt. He proclaimed his innocence. Within days, the MHA board suspended Lipscomb from his other job, and as more accusers came forward they cut off his pay.

The timing of the coup, less than six weeks from Election Day 2015, made it seem like a reprise of dirty politics from the Crump era, when physical beatings and character assassination were standard tactics. The allegations came to light as incumbent mayor A.C. Wharton battled a trio of challengers. Opinions flew about whether the city had unburdened itself of a problem or entered a leadership vacuum. Wharton lost in a landslide to Jim Strickland, who became Memphis's first white mayor since 1992.

The city now stands on the verge of a new era. Shortly before the election, HUD announced that Memphis would receive a $29.75 million Choice Neighborhood grant to demolish the city's last public housing project, Foote Homes. The feds had declined the city's application for the same project the previous year. The city replaced Foote Homes with modern townhouses, but what happens next in South Memphis is an open question.

What will happen to the neighborhood's poor, mostly black residents? What kind of community will rise in place of the old projects? Will the South Lauderdale neighborhood once again nurture leaders black and white, as it did in the early 20th century? Or will the city continue with policies and practices that have condemned African Americans to live on the wrong side of inequality?

The future begins with destruction.

CHAPTER THIRTEEN

PROTEST, POLITICS, AND PARADOX: THE BLACK FREEDOM STRUGGLE IN MEMPHIS

Aram Goudsouzian

In the epic narrative of the American civil rights movement, Memphis is the stage for tragedy. It serves as the setting for a hero's nightmarish downfall, leaving an aftermath of disillusion and defeatism. Upon the assassination of Martin Luther King Jr. on April 4, 1968, an epoch of nonviolent protest appeared dead, while Black communities quaked with grief and rage. Though the media spotlight soon turned from the city, the King assassination continues to dominate the historical memory of the Black freedom movement in Memphis. It has served as an unfortunate, abstract explanation for the city's racial polarization. But this version of the past obscures the city's complicity in its own crippled possibilities for progress. If Memphis did not kill Martin Luther King, it created the conditions that made his assassination possible.

King came to Memphis to support a strike by sanitation workers. Their protest began after a faulty compactor killed two Black workers, highlighting their terrible conditions and subservient status. The strike wove together strands in the Black community, reaching across class lines. "I've never seen a community as together as Memphis," King remarked to one associate. Throughout the winter of 1968, the protestors launched marches from Clayborn Temple and a union hall, while also picketing downtown stores and holding mass meetings. The Memphis NAACP, led by figures such as Jesse Turner and Maxine Smith, supported the strike. Activist ministers such as James Lawson lent a spirit of radical nonviolence. The Tri-State Defender and radio station WDIA articulated the justice of the workers' quest. Even a local Black Power organization known as the Invaders worked in creative, sometimes uneasy, tension with King's Southern Christian Leadership Conference.[1]

King's presence in Memphis reflected his commitment to economic justice — a broader freedom than simply winning access to public facilities and the ballot box. The city possessed a history of labor organizing. Black workers on the waterfront, in cotton processing, and the auto industry had battled against workplace discrimination and second-class citizenship. The sanitation strike was conducted through a union for public employees, the American Federation of State, County, and Municipal Employees (AFSCME). The strike thus revealed the greater possibilities for fusing labor organizing with civil rights.[2]

But the White-dominated institutions of Memphis failed its citizens. Mayor Henry Loeb refused any compromise, instead denouncing an "illegal strike." The city council hid behind the paternalist mayor. The police resorted to brutality: after a March 28 protest turned chaotic, officers fired tear gas into the church where marchers had retreated, and later killed a sixteen-year-old child named Larry Payne. The Commercial Appeal and Press-Scimitar never conveyed the perspective of the Black strikers, instead portraying noisy picketers conducting illegal actions. Moderate civic and religious leaders neither galvanized a mass of White liberal support, nor staked a firm moral ground. Thus, despite the movement's political energy and essential justice, most Whites exhibited hostility toward the strike, or at least an inability to see a Black perspective.[3]

Both the hope and heartache of 1968 had roots in the longer patterns of the city's Black freedom movement. Memphis plays a unique role in southern history. Its foundations are built on Black migrants and Black labor, but it bears the stain of racial oppression and violence. It suffers from racialized poverty, but also pulses with a vitality borne of its legacy of Black political action, Black-owned businesses, and Black cultural expression. Memphis thus straddles two worlds: urban and rural, modern and tradition-bound, culturally dynamic and socially repressive, White and Black. This paradox helps explain the resilience of Black politics and protest in Memphis, as well as the larger culture of White power that has stifled racial equality.[4]

***

Long before the sanitation strike, African Americans in Memphis engaged in political resistance to White supremacy. At the dawn of the twentieth century, Black workers helped drive the city's emergence as a center for cotton trading and lumber, even as Jim Crow laws underpinned their degraded status. After streetcars were legally segregated in 1903, they became sites to challenge injustice. Sometimes, conflicts erupted between Black and White passengers. Black passengers also filed suit against the Memphis Street Railway Company for physical injuries or verbal insults.

But Blacks also operated within a paradigm of White domination: their legal challenges tended to emphasize the plaintiffs' respectability, rather than challenge Jim Crow itself.[5]

In this same era, Memphis was stained by racial terror. In 1892, a White mob lynched Thomas Moss, the Black owner of the People's Grocery, and his two employees Calvin McDowell and Will Stewart. After a racially-charged dispute outside the store led to a shootout, the police rounded up over one hundred Blacks. A posse of Whites invaded the jail, seized the three victims, blasted shotguns into their faces, and disfigured their bodies. A White competitor took over the grocery, which had been a locus of Black pride and advancement. Such violence continued into the new century. In 1917, another mob lynched Ell Persons, a Black woodcutter unjustly accused of raping and murdering a young White woman. The horde lowered Persons' hanged body into a flaming pyre, sliced off his extremities for souvenirs, and deposited his severed head on Beale Street.[6]

African Americans responded with activism. Ida B. Wells, editor of the Free Speech, challenged Whites' notions of racial order after the People's Grocery lynching. She advocated that Blacks leave the city, blasted leaders for failing to protect Black citizens, and rejected the idea that lynching resulted from Black men raping White women. "If Southern white men are not careful," she provocatively warned, "they will overreach themselves and public sentiment will have a reaction; a conclusion will then be reached which will be very damaging to the moral reputation of their women." Wells had to flee Memphis, and her printing press was smashed. But she emerged as a worldwide crusader against lynching.[7]

After the mob killed Ell Persons, Robert Church Jr. founded the first southern branch of the NAACP. His father, Robert Church Sr., had built a real estate empire and become the region's first Black millionaire. Church Jr. would become a key middleman for national NAACP officials who investigated racial crimes in the South. Church Jr. also founded a national organization that promoted Black support of the Republican Party, known as the Lincoln League. Its conventions in Chicago in 1920 and 1924 drew masses of Republican delegates, and Church served in the integrated "black and tan" faction of the national party, with connections to President Warren Harding and Republican chairman Will Hays. Yet opposition from the "lily white" faction checked Church's ultimate influence in the Republican Party.[8]

In Memphis, Church operated within a political world shaped by Edward Hull Crump. Ruling the local Democratic machine from the 1910s into the 1950s, "Boss" Crump chose every significant city official, while holding an outsized influence on state politics. On race, Crump had a complicated impact. In Memphis, unlike in other major southern cities, African Americans voted in significant numbers. Crump courted Black votes for his preferred candidates. His machine workers rounded up voters, paid their poll taxes, and rewarded them with food and drink. A Black underworld of bootleggers and brothels thrived, so long as it operated in concert with Crump's aims. Black officials, such as Church, endorsed local Democrats and protected Crump from Republican investigation; in exchange, Blacks won political favors such as public parks, school funds, and paved streets.

But this paternalistic arrangement had limits. When the Democratic Party gained control of the White House and Congress in the 1930s, "accommodationist" Black leaders such as T.O. Fuller, Sutton Griggs, and Blair Hunt gained influence at the expense of Robert Church. Crump then drove Church out of Memphis by seeking back taxes and seizing real estate holdings. In 1940, the police department kept arresting and harassing the customers at the businesses of Church's associates, J.B. Martin and Elmer Atkinson – a campaign of racial discipline known as the "Reign of Terror."[9]

Memphis thus exhibited a degree of Black political power unique in the American South – but only in service of Boss Crump's powerful regime. This situation started changing during World War II. Black workers found opportunities, often joining labor unions and appealing to federal authorities when encountering racist hiring practices. In 1945, after two White officers sexually assaulted two Black women, African Americans rallied against police brutality. And in 1947, when Mayor James Pleasants tried to segregate audiences for a Cold War-era traveling exhibition called the "Freedom Train," Black leaders criticized this betrayal of democracy. LeMoyne College students started a new NAACP youth chapter, while White reform candidates sought Black and progressive support to challenge the Crump machine.

In 1948, Black voters helped defeat Crump's preferred candidate for Tennessee governor. In 1951, with support from Black civic clubs, J.E. Walker ran for the school board independent of the Crump machine. Three years later, Benjamin Hooks ran for the state legislature. In 1959,

Martin Luther King visited Memphis and over 57,000 African Americans registered to vote in support of an all-Black "Volunteer Ticket" that included Russell Sugarmon for public works commissioner, Benjamin Hooks for juvenile court judge, and O.Z. Evers for city commission. Though these candidates for public office lost, Black voters were shifting the political ground. In 1964 A.W. Willis became a state senator, and H.T. Lockard joined the Shelby County Court. They were the first Blacks in Tennessee to hold these positions since Reconstruction.[10]

By the early 1960s, the civil rights movement was sweeping across the South. In Memphis, the movement was shaped by the city's historic paradox as a land of both opportunity and repression. A robust NAACP branch led by middle-class professionals such as Jesse Turner, Maxine Smith, Vasco Smith, Billy Kyles, Russell Sugarmon, Benjamin Hooks, and A.W. Willis gave central direction to desegregation campaigns. White leaders, such as Mayor William Ingram and Police Commissioner Claude Armour, generally eschewed violent resistance. The Memphis Committee on Community Relations (MCCR), composed of moderate Black and White leaders, advocated measured concessions after civil rights demonstrations. Accordingly, while Blacks in Memphis engaged in energetic activism, the city avoided gory violence and national headlines.

School desegregation further revealed the nature of the Memphis movement. Following a Supreme Court ruling, Memphis State University admitted its first Black students in 1959. The "Memphis State Eight" endured isolation, lacked access to the cafeteria and student center, and needed police escorts — but there was no bloodshed along the lines of the 1962 Ole Miss Crisis, and the percentage of Black students grew over the ensuing decade. Similarly, in 1961, in response to an NAACP lawsuit, Memphis City Schools placed thirteen Black first-graders in various White elementary schools, with a plan to integrate one grade per year. It was an absurdly gradual arrangement, but the city provided good police protection. Unlike in Little Rock in 1957, no angry mobs gathered outside the schools.[11]

Black activists kept pushing for desegregation. In 1960, Owen Junior College students launched sit-ins at a downtown lunch counter, while LeMoyne College students demonstrated at Cossitt Library and other branches. The protests later spread to the Brooks Museum and public parks. The Black community populated rallies and mass meetings. As the protests continued into 1961, hundreds were arrested. Soon, legal challenges desegregated the libraries and parks, while the MCCR helped negotiate a 1962 deal with downtown merchants to integrate department stores and restaurants. That same year, the Malco movie chain hatched a desegregation plan with the NAACP. Even before to the 1964 Civil Rights Act, Memphis had integrated most of its public institutions.[12]

So Memphis earned a reputation for "good race relations." This was a double-edged sword. On one hand, the city avoided the dangerous conflicts that poisoned much of the South. On the other hand, most Black Memphians still suffered from persistent inequality, as evidenced by continued protests. High school students marched in objection to overstuffed all-Black schools and under-enrolled all-White schools. Hundreds of LeMoyne students joined the NAACP in a city hall protest against police brutality. The NAACP processed stacks of complaints of workplace discrimination for the new Equal Employment Opportunity Commission. James Lawson headed MAP-South, a federally funded anti-poverty program for job training and youth programs, and hired Charles Cabbage and Coby Smith, two young men who had founded the Black Organizing Project. These young Black Power activists emphasized Black pride, solidarity, and self-defense, while critiquing the moderate, integrationist style of the NAACP.[13]

Until 1968, however, most Whites in Memphis could ignore, or at least contain, the festering discontent among Black Memphians. Then came the sanitation strike, and the King assassination, and that was no longer possible.

***

The racial tensions that surfaced during the sanitation strike shaped its aftermath. At Memphis State University, the Black Student Association led a sit-in of the Administration Building in April 1969, demanding more Black faculty and a Black studies curriculum. That fall, the NAACP launched "Black Monday" boycotts of the school system, a protest that included mass meetings, grassroots recruiting, and an alliance with a labor strike at St. Joseph's Hospital. NAACP leaders, such as Maxine Smith, employed some of the rhetoric and tactics of Black Power.[14]

Schools served as the locus for wider debates over housing, opportunity, and city government. Starting in 1972, federal judge Robert McRae ordered busing plans to remedy the tenacious segregation in Memphis City Schools. This ruling accelerated White flight outside the city limits. There were 71,369 White students in city schools in 1973, and only

27,173 by 1980. White enrollment in private schools – including established elite prep academies, Catholic schools, new religious institutions, and ersatz schools formed by the reactionary Citizens Against Busing – quickly doubled. White parents justified these moves based on concerns about old facilities, city taxes, high crime rates, and moral decline. But racial animosities and anxieties inevitably shaped those concerns. By the early twenty-first century, racial minorities composed about 90% of students in Memphis City Schools.[15]

White flight, ironically, created new Black opportunities in the realm of electoral politics. Some called the Ford family a "mini-Crump machine." With tight organization and extensive grassroots efforts, the Fords controlled much of the Black electorate in the 1970s and 1980s. Harold Ford Sr. served in the U.S. House of Representatives from 1974 to 1996 and was succeeded by his son Harold Jr. John Ford was a longstanding state senator, and various other family members won office to the city council and Tennessee House of Representatives. Throughout this era, African Americans typically represented the three Black-majority districts on the city council, yet rarely won at-large seats, suggesting White voters' distaste for Black candidates. The city had no Black mayors during this time; while African Americans often failed to unify behind one candidate, conservatives such as Wyeth Chandler and Dick Hackett exploited racial anxieties among White voters.[16]

In 1991, W.W. Herenton became the first African American mayor of Memphis. Despite widespread White opposition, the former superintendent of Memphis City Schools engineered a consensus among Black leaders and mobilized a huge turnout in what was now a Black-majority city. He served in the office until 2009, with his support almost totally within the Black community. Race remained the key dividing line in Memphis politics. Herenton's tenure reflected not only the gains of the Black freedom struggle, but also its enduring, unrealized goals.[17]

***

In July 2016, hundreds of marchers occupied the DeSoto Bridge, shutting down the traffic crossing the Mississippi River between Arkansas and downtown Memphis. These activists were protesting not only the recent killings of Black citizens by law enforcement, but also the continued hindrances to genuine racial equality in Memphis. During a subsequent community forum with Mayor Jim Strickland, Black Memphians asked questions about improving schools, curbing police brutality, investing in job training and youth programs, and raising wages. A long freedom struggle had delivered electoral power. It had desegregated facilities and institutions. It had led to Black public officials. And it had created educational and economic opportunities for some — but not all. As of 2013, one-third of Black Memphians lived in poverty. Memphis had the highest rates of child poverty and infant mortality of any comparable city in the United States.[18]

If these are thick and sticky problems, they are also problems that require new public policies and a moral reorientation — including a recognition that "Black lives matter." Black Memphians have fought for such ends throughout their history. That fight continues.

CHAPTER FOURTEEN

BEAUTY AND BITTERNESS:
TWO CENTURIES OF MEMPHIS EDUCATION

Daniel Kiel

On October 3, 1961, four first graders walked to school. A set of twins, Sheila and Sharon Malone flanked their mother, who stood tall and upright as she accompanied her girls across the street, her eyes fixed forward. Behind them, young Alvin Freeman held on to his own mother's hand as they stepped off the curb on their way to Gordon Elementary. At the front of the group, little Pamela Mayes was also holding onto a hand as she walked, that of lawyer Russell Sugarmon, who had worked so hard to make this moment happen.

Though the school year had started weeks before, Pamela, Alvin, Sharon, and Sheila were walking to a new school that morning. These first graders, along with peers at three other elementary schools, were to be the first Black students to attend Memphis schools that had previously been reserved for White students. It was their parents who had volunteered them and local lawyers and civil rights leaders who had fought to make this happen, but it would be thirteen first graders who would desegregate schools in Memphis.

In Memphis' first two centuries, hundreds of thousands of children have walked into a huge variety of schools. Stretching into the past from that morning in 1961 were decades of change tracing back all the way to the small log cabin in Court Square that opened as the city's first recorded educational institution in the 1830s.[1] Memphis education evolved along with the city, through war and disease, industrialization and migration. The schooling system of 1961 would have been barely recognizable to the earliest Memphians. Ever-present, however, until the morning thirteen Black first graders entered four new schools, was the separation of students by race. Something changed that morning.

Nearly six decades have passed and though they could not see it at the time, the future of Memphis education stretched ahead of the city's little civil rights pioneers as well. The city's education system would continue to reflect the story of Memphis. The question of racial equality would remain, but other questions would emerge as well: questions about poverty, the effects of suburbanization, the best way to educate students on the technological new frontier of the twenty-first century.

From its origins to its contemporary state, two currents have animated the Memphis education story. One has been the challenge of equality in a racially, ethnically, socioeconomically, geographically diverse community. Every advance in Memphis education was accompanied by questions of which students to serve and how. Most vexing has been the challenge of racial segregation and the ongoing struggle to ensure equity in educational opportunities across racial lines, but the challenge has not been limited to race. Students from a multitude of ethnic backgrounds, students with disabilities, and students of different religions have also had to confront the durable obstacles of exclusion and discrimination.

But equally present is another current that has animated Memphis education beyond the desegregation struggle: a belief that education could serve as the foundation for a community. For generations of Memphians of all races, hope has been placed in the idea that an education can not only engender good habits of citizenship, but can also empower individuals to find their passions and reach their potential. Paradoxically, it is this hope that makes schools central battlegrounds in struggles for social change, as all recognize the power of education to impact a community's future. The record of delivering on this hope in the power of education is decidedly mixed, since there are as many failures as successes, but the hope remains. It was evident in the rudimentary schools opened to serve young (White) Memphians during the city's earliest years and in the desire among parents and civil rights leaders to break down the inequitable schooling structures of Jim Crow. And it remains evident in the centrality of education within contemporary public discussion and the continuing efforts to make education both more effective and more equitable.

There is both beauty and bitterness in this story, as there is in the city itself.

ORIGINS OF EDUCATION IN MEMPHIS

The belief in the role education might play in shaping the future of Memphis was present from the beginning, as the city's initial charter provided for the establishment of public schools.[2] The city's earliest education took place in less formal establishments, but in the 1840s, the outlines of the education environment that would carry into the twentieth century came into focus. The all-girls school that would become St. Mary's Episcopal School was founded in 1847. In 1848, the city's Board of Mayor and Alderman opened the first public schools for White children between the ages of six and sixteen.[3] On the eve of the Civil War, in addition to a series of small, religious schools, the city operated 21 schools serving more than a thousand White students.[4]

Black children were excluded from such formal schooling by virtue of ordinances prohibiting education of slaves, though some received informal education at home. The small number of children of free Blacks were also excluded from the city's public schools.[5] The conclusion of the Civil War brought with it not only emancipation for Black Memphians, but also schooling, demonstrating the hope that increased education could help lift the newly-emancipated population. Schools for Black children were opened by the Freedmen's Bureau and by aid societies. In the late 1860s, the city opened the first public school for Black Memphians, the Clay Street School, which would eventually come to be known as Booker T. Washington High School.

Such advances, however, were met with violent resistance as the power of education to transform the existing social order threatened local White supremacy. In the 1866 Memphis Massacre, Black schools were targeted during the riots; twelve such schools were destroyed and one student was killed.[6] Such resistance to any progress toward improved Black education would be repeated a century later in the years following the entrance of those thirteen first graders into formerly White schools in 1961. Antipathy toward the education of Black Memphians has stalked the halls of history.

By the early twentieth century, school had become compulsory for the community's youth. Private religious and independent schools, including some, like the Rosenwald schools, created to serve Black students, existed alongside free schools. Public schools were split in multiple ways — the Memphis City Schools served those residing in the city, while the Shelby County Schools served students in the rural county. Both public districts segregated students by race as required by both state and local law. The Supreme Court decision in Brown v. Board of Education in 1954 declaring racial segregation in schools to be unconstitutional disrupted this status quo and triggered the events that would lead to those thirteen Black students desegregating the schools.

THE MEMPHIS 13 AND INTEGRATION

The initial desegregation of the Memphis City Schools in October 1961 was not the most impactful moment in the history of education in Memphis. After all, it only involved four schools, and thirteen Black students, their families, their teachers, and their dozens of White classmates. At the time, there were nearly 100,000 students in the city schools and thousands more in either private schools or Shelby County Schools.[7] The story nonetheless represented the first cracks in a long-existing social order that kept Memphians separated by skin color. It also demonstrated the hope that Memphis might navigate racial difficulties and emerge as a model for a successful, diverse city. However, the limits of that hope were lamentably evident in the story that followed the initial desegregation, with many White families leaving schools or leaving the entire system, opting for private schools or the growing suburban school system beyond city lines. The common belief in the power of education to shape a community can be seen in both the idealism of starting with children to change a community and the resistance to that change.

On an individual level, the thirteen Black students and their White classmates were among the first people in Memphis to coexist in a multi-racial setting as equals. Many of the students created friendships across racial lines, though there was no shortage of antagonism as well. Teachers demonstrated their power within the education story in ways both helpful and hurtful. Students drew varied lessons from their trailblazing experiences: some left with a belief in their own ability to succeed anywhere, while others felt the sting of inequality even in a desegregated environment.

In response to the 1954 Brown decision, MCS Board President Milton Bowers insisted that no changes would be needed: "We believe our Negroes will continue using their own facilities since most of them are in the center of Negro population areas."[8] Yet, as the 1950s came to a close, the viability of maintaining absolute segregation had eroded. In 1957, the federal government made clear that it would not tolerate obstruction when it used troops to enforce the desegregation of Little Rock's Central High School. The Little Rock story, and the accompanying crisis, loomed large on the minds of Memphis officials as events moved inexorably toward desegregation. Though the local NAACP had initiated a desegregation lawsuit, Northcross v. Board of Education, and the School Board resisted all pressure to loosen existing racial barriers, both the White city establishment and local civil rights leaders wished to avoid the ugly confrontations of Little Rock. Tentative as it was, there was coordination across racial lines in arranging to break the color line in public schools.

During the summer of 1961, the school board began developing general policies for desegregation, while local NAACP leaders recruited Black parents willing to apply for their children to transfer into White schools. Several weeks into the school year, the requests of thirteen of the applicants were granted. With desegregation looming, the city's White establishment worked to ensure order even if its support for the Brown decision was less than enthusiastic. In an official statement on the day the students desegregated schools in Memphis, the Mayor and City Commission noted, "Many people feel that the decision of the Supreme Court declaring school segregation unlawful was ill-timed and ill-advised...[But] The Mayor and the City Commissioners...emphasize that the desegregation of our schools must be and will be accomplished free of unrest or violence. No other course will be tolerated."[9]

On the morning of October 3, a visible police presence ensured there would be no large, public incidents, and the local NAACP leaders accompanied the brave children to an extraordinary day of school. According to the official reports, Memphis took school desegregation "in stride."[10] The official interracial cooperation offered a glimpse of the city's potential to navigate its grueling racial terrain.

The students themselves, however, did not experience the official version of events – as Sheila Malone recalled, "Once those doors closed and our parents walked out of that school, it was us."[11] One of the first things the students noticed was the disparity between their new schools and their old ones. Though there was great pride in the city's historic Black schools, such as Booker T. Washington and Manassas, the system of segregation ensured that resources were not equally shared. Remembering her first days at Gordon, Sheila Malone quipped, "I thought I'd died and gone to heaven." Joyce White, who desegregated Rozelle Elementary along with three other children, recalled her surprise that the "the books were crispy new."[12]

One of the motivations for using first graders rather than high school students was a belief among the NAACP leadership that younger children would not experience the same type of racial antagonism as high schoolers might. Indeed, some of the Black students did develop interracial friendships. Jacqueline Moore, who desegregated Springdale Elementary, recalled two little girls who made her feel welcome from day one, and Pamela Mayes ascribed a lifelong lack of prejudice to her friendship with two White siblings, Helen and Chris.[13]

However, these earliest days of racial coexistence were not without difficulty. Though order reigned outside of the schools, many of the students were often reminded that their presence threatened the existing social order. Pamela recalled that once her relationship with Helen and Chris became known, a group of other students jumped her and beat her up. This first grader was getting a powerful education about the beauty of interracial friendship and the bitterness of racial animosity.[14] As the desegregation story continued to unfold over the coming years, that contrast would become increasingly evident outside of the schools as well.

TOWARD CONTEMPORARY MEMPHIS EDUCATION

By 1970, the process that began with thirteen first graders had spread to upend more than a century of racial segregation in schools. Within Memphis City Schools, 101 of the district's 155 schools had at least one student of a different race.[15] In 1963, Jesse Turner, the son of a local civil rights leader, had become the first Black student to attend a formerly White high school, public or private, when he entered Christian Brothers High.[16] Student protests, known as Black Mondays, had led to the election of the first African American school board member, Maxine Smith. Students in a variety of environments were experiencing an education that spoke to the hope of a Memphis delivering excellent and equitable opportunities for all.

But progress was limited. In 1970, there remained 54 single-race public schools in the city and though most schools were technically "desegregated," the vast majority of students were still learning in largely racially homogenous environments. For example, 89% of Black students and 81% of White students were still in schools that were more than 90% made up of students of a single-race.[17] In the Shelby County Schools, which were involved in a desegregation lawsuit of their own, only 1.3% of the district's Black students were attending predominantly White schools.[18] Racially separate learning remained the norm, lessening the impact of the educational revolution.

Consequently, the fight to expand desegregation that took place in the early 1970s *was* the moment that has most shaped the last half century of Memphis schooling. In 1973, after surveying the landscape of the racial makeup of the Memphis City Schools, Judge Robert McRae ordered a plan for busing tens of thousands of students that he termed "Plan Z" in hopes that it would end local desegregation litigation.[19] In a way, it did. This order, which came over a decade after the first thirteen students had desegregated schools, and nearly two decades since the 1954 *Brown* decision, aimed to override the official intransigence of the school board in creating schools that reflected the racial diversity of the city and school district.

The prospect of busing threatened to disrupt the racially-separate status quo even more than the early years of desegregation and responses were varied. There were those, Black and White, who thought it a necessary order to ensure equal educational opportunities to all Memphis students. Within the Black community, there were others who had tired of the focus on desegregation and wished for greater resources for schools that continued to serve a largely African American student population. Within the White community, there were those who resented having school choices imposed upon them, many of whom found the prospect of being bused to historically Black schools unacceptable. This final group fueled the engine of "White flight" in Memphis. Their numbers were evident in the decrease in White enrollment in Memphis City Schools from 42% to 32% within a year. Over the course of a summer, the district lost a third of its White student population. Students poured into newly-formed private schools or the increasingly suburban and rapidly expanding Shelby County Schools. Private school enrollment nearly doubled between 1972 and 1973 and the Shelby County Schools would embark on a lengthy period of growth even as the city periodically annexed unincorporated portions of the county.[20]

By the end of the 1970s, the dust had largely settled on the era of desegregation. Busing had become largely ineffectual due to the exodus of White students. The district shifted attention to increasing educational quality through "optional" schools that provided enhanced programming. By the turn of the twenty-first century, most students, regardless of whether they attended public or private, city or county schools, were in racially-identifiable learning environments. This was not imposed by law, as it had been a century earlier, but very few Memphians learned in environments that reflected the community's broad and increasing diversity. Black students dominated all but a handful of Memphis City Schools, including several of the district's well-reputed optional schools. Even the city's increasing Latino population found itself concentrated in only a few of the city's schools. Meanwhile, most private schools served predominantly (through rarely exclusively) White student populations. The suburban public schools continued to reflect the majority-White populations outside of Memphis' boundaries.

But racial and ethnic makeup of schools tells only part of the Memphis education story. In each generation, dynamic students emerged from all sorts of schooling environments, evincing a depth of talent and industry capable of impacting the world. However, on a systemic basis, the city's racially-isolated schooling was persistently accompanied by racially disparate educational opportunities. The same inequality that once drove the parents of thirteen first graders to seek enrollment in schools with "crispy new" books continued to plague education in Memphis.

By virtually every measure, from pre-school literacy rates to college readiness, from disciplinary action to access to a rigorous curriculum, Memphis education remained riddled with racial disparities. These disparities in quality acted as a drag on the promise of education and strangled the hope that talented and industrious individuals would be equipped with opportunities to succeed. The continued correlation between race and educational opportunity revealed the extent to which Memphis education had fallen short on this promise in its first two centuries.

And the demoralizing message could not have been lost on students, who understand when the odds are stacked against them. Looking back at his experience as a pioneering student at Rozelle Elementary, Clarence Williams declared, "The knowledge I gained from going to that school was that I was not equal...I knew where my place was in life. I felt that from an early age."[21] The danger of such lessons remains as present as Memphis enters its third century as it was in 1961.

INTO THE THIRD CENTURY

In December 2010, the educational landscape in Memphis encountered yet another disruption. This time, facing long-term fiscal vulnerability, the Memphis City Schools dissolved its charter, triggering a period of administrative uncertainty that included the possibility that the district would merge with the suburban Shelby County Schools to create a single county-wide school district. District consolidation had long simmered beneath the surface of public debate about the future of the metropolitan area, but vigorous resistance from outside of the city limits prevented any plan from gaining traction. The city district's radical charter surrender, however, pushed the issue to the top of the community's consciousness.

The potential merger again challenged a status quo that kept local students separate from one another, this time administratively. Layered together were the wounds of the past and the community's lingering racial challenges. Memphis City Schools was led by an African American superintendent, governed by a majority-Black school board, and served a student population that was over 90% students of color, including 85% African American. In contrast, Shelby County Schools had a White superintendent, an all-White school board, and a diverse, but majority-White (52%) student population.[22]

The potential district merger occurred within an already-changing education landscape. There remained the public and private options, an expanded number of optional school programs within Memphis City Schools, and the now-fluid line between city and county schools. But in addition, a new breed of public school, charter schools that were privately-operated but publicly-funded, was serving a growing number of local students. Some of these schools were even operated by a newly-created state school district that was given the task of turning around unsuccessful schools. These reforms were part of a broader effort to improve the overall quality of education that included focus on the community's teachers and early childhood education. By the mid 2010s, Memphis had become a national hub of education reform, a testament both to the immense need for improvement and the belief in the importance of education.

Ultimately, the voices of resistance to a consolidated district won out. After a single year of a county-wide school district, the local education landscape fractured with six newly-created suburban municipal districts alongside a new incarnation of Shelby County Schools serving students in Memphis. Thus, Memphis would enter its third century with a different name for its largest school system, but a familiarly divided landscape.

If racial separation was the dominant issue of educational equity during the city's first 200 years, the most pressing educational challenge today is poverty. Poverty plays a confounding role in education, creating a vicious cycle for a community. Students growing up in poverty face physical, psychological, and educational challenges stemming from the scarcity in their lives. In Memphis, this problem is immense. The city's overall child poverty rate was 34.5% in 2016. For African American children, the poverty rate was 48.3%.[23] It is worth noting that this stubbornly high poverty rate exists despite vast increases in the levels of educational attainment within the Black community; high school graduation rates have jumped from 9% in 1960, on the eve of the city's initial school desegregation, to over 85% in 2016.[24]

Yet, educational challenges are not only caused by poverty; they are also a cause of persistent poverty. Earnings rise with levels of education, meaning that those who are unsuccessful in school are more likely to have lower incomes and to raise children in poverty.[25] This cycle of educational failure and poverty threatens to cripple a community across generations and constitutes the biggest challenge for Memphis today.

But if the structures of Memphis education remain bitterly flawed, the beauty of education's potential to shape individual futures is on display every school day. Students from all different types of racial, religious, and socioeconomic backgrounds, students from all over the city, students in all types of schools, arrive each day to learn from hard-working teachers amidst the hope that their successes will be the community's successes. It has been that way from the simple beginnings of Memphis education through its evolution to today's complex series of schools serving over 100,000 students in a diverse set of environments. As Romanita Morris, a parent of one of the Memphis 13, put it to her son, Harry Williams: "You go get your education; you can be anything you want to be."[26]

CHAPTER FIFTEEN

THE TIGERS, THE GRIZZLIES, AND THE CITY WE WISH TO BE

Geoff Calkins

Like so much that was wonderful about the Memphis Grizzlies extended playoff run in 2015, the moment just happened; it was organic, totally unplanned. The Grizzlies had just beaten Portland in Game 2 of their playoff series. Happy fans spilled out onto the FedExForum plaza. The band started playing the "Cupid Shuffle," that cheesy tune you hear at a lot of wedding receptions. And all of a sudden, people started to dance.

At first, it was just a handful of people. Then a handful became dozens. Then dozens became hundreds. And suddenly it felt like half the population of Memphis was doing a line dance downtown.

Young people and old people were out there dancing. Black people and White people were out there dancing. Some of the dancers looked like they hadn't danced a day in their lives.

A video of the moment went viral. The same spring another video had gone viral in Memphis, of a group of kids pummeling shoppers in a Kroger parking lot. This video could not have been more different than that one. It captured the best of Memphis. It captured a much more typical Memphis. Just a bunch of people, good-hearted people, getting along and laughing at their missteps and celebrating their city and their lives.

Memphians like to say that sports bring people together in this often-fragmented town. They say it so much that it has become a cliché. And, of course, there are limits to how much sports really brings together, and how meaningful that togetherness really is. Wendi Thomas, the former columnist for The Commercial Appeal, wrote a piece for The Undefeated headlined, "Stop using basketball as a Band-Aid for racial progress." In the piece, Thomas wrote, "Yes, the crowds at Grizzlies games are more racially mixed than probably any other setting in town. But proximity is not proof of progress, no matter what civic boosters want to believe. In virtually all measures that matter — rates of homeownership, poverty, income, graduation and wealth — black Americans lag behind white Americans. And in some measures, like wealth, the black-white gap is growing."[1]

Thomas is right about all this, of course. Sports is not a cure for broader social ills. That is as true in Memphis as it is everywhere else. The diversity of the crowd at Grizzlies games does not excuse the lack of diversity in our public schools. The fact that Black and White fans happily blend together at FedExForum does undo the racial and economic stratification that continues to define this town.

"God bless the Grizzlies and their commemorative MLK jerseys, they are a thing of beauty," Thomas told me in 2017. "But if MLK were here, he wouldn't give a flip about jerseys, he just wouldn't. He was a radical, he was a prophet, and I think he'd have a lot to say about the state of economic justice today."

Agreed. Sports is neither a quick fix nor a panacea. It should not be seen as such. But I would argue that sports, and the way we talk about our favorite sports stories, can reflect our highest aspirations, our sense of what we want our community to be. And in Memphis, our two favorite sports stories are about two basketball teams that each, in their own way, and in their own time, reflected our desire to be a better version of ourselves.

The first story is about Larry Finch, the kid from Orange Mound, who remains the most important player in Memphis basketball history. Finch may not have been the greatest player. Some would argue on behalf of Penny Hardaway or Keith Lee. But he was indisputably the most important player, because of the impact he had on the city in the tense and polarized years that followed the assassination of Martin Luther King Jr. in April of 1968.

In 1968, Finch was a burgeoning star at Melrose High School. His mother, Maple Finch, earned $5.50 a day cleaning houses — the 50¢ was to pay for bus fare. Finch developed his skills on the playgrounds of Orange Mound. He had a jump shot that was even sweeter than his smile.

But when it came time to decide where to go to college, Finch was faced with a dilemma. Many in the African American community, including Williams Collins, his coach at Melrose, did not want him to go to what was then called Memphis State. Until 1964, the university did not permit coaches to recruit black athletes. A long list of gifted basketball players had been forced to leave the city to play college ball. Bobby Smith, an extraordinarily talented player who went on to have a long NBA career, had signed with Memphis in 1965, but was subsequently denied admission.

"People didn't trust Memphis State," said Leonard Draper, who got to know Finch from his work at a local community center. "There was a lot of pressure on him to go somewhere else. There was a lot of heat. But Larry wanted to stay home. He wanted to be close to his mother. He loved Memphis. I told him that if his heart told him to go to Memphis State he should follow his heart. I think it turned out okay."

Finch scored his first basket — a 25-foot jumper — six seconds into his first varsity game. He went on to score 1,859 points over three seasons and to lead Memphis State to the national championship game. But it says something about that time and about Finch's enduring impact that Memphians who lived through the Finch era talk less about what he accomplished than what it meant. That is not the way most athletes are remembered. They are remembered for their records or their rings. Cal Ripken's 2,632 consecutive games. Tom Brady's six Super Bowl titles. Finch is remembered for something larger and more meaningful. He is remembered for helping Memphis heal.

This was a Memphis that was driven by a court-ordered busing program. This was a Memphis that saw thousands of white students leave the school system in response. In Zack McMillin's definitive series on the 1972-1973 Tigers that ran in The Commercial Appeal in 2003, McMillin noted that the day before Finch's first varsity game, the city council met with New York Times publisher Arthur Ochs Sulzberger, who asked the council members to identify the city's biggest problem. The answer: racial divisions.

"There is as much polarization at the grass roots level as ever, maybe more," said James L. Netters, a council member. "One serious event, one big event could ignite it again."[2]

Finch and the Tigers provided a respite from all that. A point of community pride. "I remember sitting on my floor and watching him play," said Hank McDowell, who would go on to star for the Tigers and now does commentary on the radio broadcasts. "We didn't know he was bringing the city together or anything. We were just all cheering for the same team."

They cheered Memphis State all the way to the Final Four in St. Louis, where the Tigers defeated Providence to earn the right to play Bill Walton and UCLA. If there's one thing Memphians remember about that game — besides Bill Walton hitting twenty-one of twenty-two shots and scoring forty-four points — it's the way the city felt while it was taking place. Memphis was a ghost town. The happiest sort of ghost town. Nobody was out driving around, because everyone was watching TV.

"Man, it was like 'Shout Hallelujah," said Wyeth Chandler, the mayor in 1973. "The entire town could finally just sit back and enjoy something together."[3]

It almost didn't matter that Memphis State didn't win the title. Finch and his teammates had given their community something to hold onto during a tumultuous and potentially explosive time. No, they didn't solve any of the underlying issues of racism and poverty. Of course, they didn't do that. Nor did Billie Jean King create instant equality between the sexes when she defeated Bobby Riggs in a tennis match a few months after the Memphis-UCLA championship game. But Finch's story still resonates in Memphis more than four decades later, because those who watched it unfold understood the very real impact it had. Rick Spell, a Memphis booster who was a student at the time, told McMillin that he has watched prominent Memphians struggle just to put that impact into words. "You can see they are describing an emotion that the other person doesn't quite understand," Spell said. "And these are very large people. Allen Morgan and Pitt Hyde and those types of people. That was a big moment for them."[4] Former Memphis Tiger Mike Butler, who passed away in November of 2018, put it even more simply. "They changed hearts and minds," he said.[5]

That's what sports figures can do, at their best. They can challenge the way we see the world and ourselves, which brings us to the city's other favorite sports story: the story of the grit and grind Memphis Grizzlies. When news first broke that the Vancouver Grizzlies were thinking of moving to Memphis, people were genuinely shocked. The city had been trying to lure an NFL team for decades. When the Houston Oilers moved to Nashville, the dream of becoming a major league city appeared to have been crushed for good. It was a blow to the civic psyche. It fed into the city's much-ballyhooed inferiority complex. At the time, nobody was more critical of Memphis than Memphians, and at least some of that negative sentiment can be traced back to the decades of rejection by the NFL.

Enter the Pursuit Team, a small group of philanthropic Memphians who decided to try to bring an NBA franchise to town. Some owners of sports teams were motivated by ego. Others were motivated by a desire to hang out with stars. These Memphians, Pitt Hyde and Staley Cates being the most prominent among them, were motivated by a desire to bring something to Memphis that everyone could rally around. Seriously. That was it. The Grizzlies may be the only professional sports franchise that came into existence with community-building as an explicit goal.

Naturally, the cynics didn't believe this. There was a massive civic fight over whether to spend $250 million in public funds to build FedExForum. If the issue had been put to a referendum, which is what arena opponents wanted, the referendum would have almost certainly failed. Yard signs were planted all over town that said, "No Taxes NBA." County Commissioner Morris Fair voted in favor of the arena and, because of that vote, lost his next race.

For the longest time, the Grizzlies struggled on the court as well. Attendance was mediocre. The three years the Grizzlies made it into the playoffs, they were swept out without winning a game. Rumors persisted that the franchise would up and leave town. Never mind that the terms of the arena lease made it clear that the Grizzlies weren't going anywhere. That civic inferiority complex could manifest itself in irrational ways.

Then Mike Conley, Marc Gasol, Zach Randolph, and Tony Allen arrived in town. And everything changed. Those players are now known as the Core Four. At the time they were a collection of misfits who weren't expected to do much. Conley was considered the booby prize of the 2007 NBA draft, the player the Grizzlies had to settle for after missing out on Greg Oden and Kevin Durant. Gasol was known as Pau's fat little brother, the kid who weighed a whopping 350 pounds during his time at Lausanne. Randolph had been bounced from the Trail Blazers to the Knicks to the Clippers because of character issues. Some idiot columnist — okay, it was me — wrote that trading for Randolph would be a serious mistake. And Allen was so lightly regarded by his old team, the Boston Celtics, that they let him walk to Memphis as a free agent.

Together, these players changed a franchise, and in the process they changed a city, too. "Grit and Grind" became a civic mantra. Randolph explained, "We don't bluff." The team printed up tens of thousands of growl towels that said, "Believe, Memphis" and, sure enough, people did. They believed. In Memphis. And not just in the basketball team. They believed that this scrappy, under-appreciated, big-hearted river town would find a way to harness the energy and creativity of its citizens to meet its many needs.

It was astonishing to watch it unfold. The same people who once argued against bringing the franchise to Memphis, because it would surely leave — that was their actual logic — now named their dogs Z-Bo or Big Spain. Memphians turned their growl towels into neckties and wore them to church. They stuck a headband on Le Bonheur's giant heart logo. St. Jude Children's Research Hospital hung a giant growl towel that said, "We believe."

It was more authentic than any Elvis impersonator and more organic, too. Not since the Showtime Lakers had an NBA team more accurately reflected a city's character. And the whole world knew Los Angeles was Showtime before that version of the Lakers. Suddenly, the world knew that Memphis grinds. That it has a chip on its shoulder as big as the river that separates it from Arkansas. "Do we have a chip on our shoulder? Yes, we do," said AC Wharton, who was mayor during the deepest playoff runs. "I have a chip on my shoulder. Whenever I got into a room representing Memphis I have a chip on my shoulder and I dare anyone to knock it off."

As with Larry Finch's Memphis State team, it hardly mattered that the Grizzlies didn't win a title. That wasn't the point. Chris Herrington, my colleague at *The Daily Memphian* put it beautifully after Gasol was traded to the Toronto Raptors, effectively ending the era of the Core Four. "I once compared them to an earlier Memphis group, Stax Records house band Booker T. & the MGs," Herrington wrote. "The fit was near-perfect: Randolph and Gasol were the rhythm section, with the racial roles reversed. Gasol, like drummer Al Jackson Jr., sat at the back, looking out for his teammates and keeping things on beat. Randolph, like bassist Duck Dunn, provided a low-end thump. Conley, like organist/bandleader Booker T. Jones, was a soft-spoken, steadying presence, a conductor of sorts, who let others shine. And Tony Allen, like guitarist Steve Cropper, was always riffing creatively off to the side, adding essential color and character to his bandmates' deep groove.

"Good bands and good basketball teams can serve a similar cultural function: To dramatize community. To show how individuals can find their best selves, their fullest expression, in service to and in cooperation with others. Each of these respective groups of MGs struck a deeper chord, one that felt more personal and more specific to the city in which they formed and in which they created. With the Grit and Grind Grizzlies, the racial dynamics inherent in Booker T. & the MGs went a step further. There was a class dimension too. Allen and Randolph, from Chicago's South Side and rough-and-tumble Marion, Indiana, respectively, balanced by Gasol, of beautiful Barcelona and Lausanne Collegiate School, and by son-of-an-Olympian Conley."[6]

Memphians saw themselves in the Grizzlies. And what they saw was good. People still say that Memphis has an inferiority complex, but it's more out of habit at this point than anything else. It's no longer actually true. Memphians snap up all manner of local pride T-shirts. They pose for selfies in front of the "I Love Memphis" mural and they invariably Choose 901. The new professional soccer team even has 901 embedded in its name: Memphis 901 FC. Indeed, one can argue that Memphians are now at times guilty of civic boosterism. But given where the city came from, that is welcome excess.

The night before the county commission voted on whether to build FedExForum, Channel 5 televised a public debate on the issue. An arena opponent named Heidi Shafer said her resistance to the deal could be summarized in two words: "Sidney Shlenker." Shlenker was the man who had failed to deliver on all his elaborate promises about The Pyramid, the arena that has since been turned into a gigantic Bass Pro store. The Pyramid was considered a civic boondoggle. Shlenker's name had become such a powerful symbol of failure that it was invoked as an argument against bringing an NBA team to town. But it wasn't an argument as much a shorthand summary of civic fear.

We've screwed up before. We'll screw up again. We should never try anything grand. The NBA will fail in Memphis. We don't support anything anyway. This is Memphis, after all. Capital city of the botched job. We produced Mud Island. We produced The Pyramid. And, yeah, in case you forgot, we produced Sidney Shlenker.

Happily, the county commission rejected that line of thinking. And nearly two decades of later, that sort of civic self-loathing has been replaced by a gritty pride. While the Grizzlies certainly aren't the sole reason for this, they have become its most visible and entertaining symbol. The "No Taxes NBA" signs that were once planted in front yards across the city were replaced by Grizzlies yard hearts — wooden, heart-shaped Grizzly logos, painted by a teenager named Donte Davis, to raise money for the Carpenter Art Garden.

Jimmy Keep, an 89-year-old Iwo Jima vet who was honored by the franchise, explained that Randolph was his favorite player because he is "not afraid to bust your ass."[7] Jade Rogers, a 24-year-old Grizzlies fan with cerebral palsy, said she watched Grizzlies' highlights on her laptop whenever she grew discouraged with the trials of her everyday life. "I'll think how hard they work even if they're tired," she said. "I'll remind myself, 'If they can do it, I can do it, too.'"[8]

The Grizzlies are just a basketball team, of course. Just as the 1972-1973 Memphis Tigers were just a basketball team. And it's easy to overstate their significance in the grand scheme of things. But both teams, in different ways, gave Memphians reason to believe in the future of their city at time when that belief had worn thin. Belief isn't the answer to everything, of course. It can't be ill-founded or naive. But without it, how is anything else possible? It's a beginning, not an end.

That's why it matters when the whole city does the Cupid Shuffle, when hundreds of strangers find themselves moving together out of unselfconscious giddiness and joy. Basketball can't solve the deeper problems of the city. It can't fix poverty or crime. But over the decades, it has proven to have an uncanny ability to move us in the right direction, one dance step at a time.

CHAPTER SIXTEEN

REAL MUSEUMS OF MEMPHIS

Zandria F. Robinson

I wasn't well able enough to be a live and in-person witness to the April 4th celebration/commemoration/reflection of/upon the life, lynching, and legacy of Dr. Martin Luther King, Jr. in Memphis. I don't know how long my sickness had been creeping, but I took note of it several Fridays ago, when I stood on my porch and watched the red-lettered "I AM MEMPHIS" slogan float onto my street all tall and blaring on the side of a sanitation truck on pickup day. "Who is Memphis?" I snapped at no one in particular, adjusting my raggedy pink flannel robe and my bonnet because I had been so assaulted by the declaration. The sound of my voice hit the street and a "Shiiiid, sista, Ion'teeno" bounced back from a sanitation worker grabbing up and dumping the contents of green cans. I waved weakly in the direction of the voice, and whispered a "mane" in response, and then, more definitively, a "THANK, Y'ALL!" as the truck and its logo made its way on down the street.

Lately Memphis been engaged in a kind of gross boosterism that prefigures the spectacular simulacra that is MLK50. There is a new Memphis afoot, built on the post-racial capitalist fantasy of "grit and grind," that aims to attract new Memphians to teach in the rapidly expanding charter school sector, to endow our country town with the sophisticated art cultures they bring as they flee the rising rents in their better cities, and to innovate new ways for more new Memphians to live off poverty via the city's expansive foundation and non-profit landscape. In exchange, the city rewards these new Memphians for their sacrifices, for living in such a poor Black town, with no sufficient public transportation to reduce their carbon footprints, where good coffee and cocktails and neighborhood bars are only just coming into reach, by highlighting their valiant choice of Memphis as their new home. There are institutes and trainings and leadership seminars for these new Memphians, where they learn their role in and worth to the city, as well as all of the requisite statistics about infant mortality rates (answer: get well-meaning white women to help Black pregnant people love themselves!), food deserts (answer: grow your own food, Blacks!), and health disparities (answer: bike lanes!). Beyond the usual tensions between the tourist version of a city and the "real" city, this new Memphis, which perhaps is the real cause of all our sickness, obliterates now Memphis and buries then Memphis, in all of its complexity and depth, at the Lorraine Motel.

The fiftieth anniversary of the assassination of Martin Luther King, Jr., is to Memphis what the Olympics was to Atlanta over 20 years ago, which is about right for how many years we are behind Atlanta in other things. As communities have been reshaped, neglected, obscured, and obliterated in the lead-up to this moment, and as they will continue to be from here on out, we have to assess that then Memphis. We also have to tell the world loudly about the now Memphis, tell it straight from the mouths of the people whose necks the now Memphis, like the then Memphis, keeps its foot on. And we have to keep track of how our memories and experiences are being gentrified in a notion of progress that has no meaningful proof or original referent.

The discursive destruction of then Memphis and now Memphis ain't start when I saw that sanitation truck, of course. It started 27 years previous, when the National Civil Rights Museum opened that July and the city of Memphis finally elected its first Black mayor (right on time, almost 20 years after Atlanta) that October. There was a museum about our history, about American history, and a Black mayor. It was Obama and the Blacksonian before Obama and the Blacksonian were a twinkle in the chocolate city's eye.

I was nine when the Museum opened, which meant I was already 23 years into the mourning that got in everybody's blood within a 25-mile radius that Thursday evening, April 4, 1968. That mourning had gotten in our blood so much so that the next generation of folks who bore babies here were more likely to lose they babies than anyone else in any other city in this country. Being born with an extra 14 years of mourning, plus learning in your own nine years just as soon as you could comprehend your own name what you should know about that mourning, and why you had to carry it just as you carried yourself—so tall and proud and better than the worst of you and the worst of white folks, too—made me tired before I ever even could really know tiredness. Like Fannie Lou Hamer sick-and-tired-of-being-sick-and-tired kind of tired. The kind of tired that made me extra musty as a little girl for no apparent reason.

The Museum was added to our annual school field trip rotation alongside trips to the zoo, which, thanks to the miracle of desegregation, we could now go to any day we pleased. We went on His birthday, on free

Tuesdays, during Black History Month, and sometimes for the anniversary, and sometimes because we were on the civil rights unit in social studies. I came to expect the funkiest feeling in my heart and stomach when we got to the bus and Rosa Parks and the bus driver and the other sculptural figures were still sitting there in silent history. I hoped Ms. Parks got up in the night after the museum was closed, put her makeup on to bring her color in good, got up from her seat, and marched up the aisle and slapped the dog shit out that bus driver. Every time I returned to the Museum, to that bus, there was no evidence that she had done any such thing. I jumped at the bus driver in the way we thrust our shoulders forward and furrowed our brows to threaten a fight on the blacktop.

"My Mama was alive during them times," I whispered not quietly to classmates on those trips, nodding with a practiced gravity. That museum told me them times was over. I wish that museum had told me that these was them times. My Mama Museum told me that these was still them times, and that them times would always be these times as long as we were Black and alive, and probably even after we were Black and dead. I hadn't yet registered that I arrived in this life with 14 years of mourning that, like the stank of my right underarm, told me that these was them times. Sometimes I felt silly for thinking that these times was them times, because there weren't dogs and hoses and nooses and crosses burning and white women's teeth. Then I felt silly for ignoring all the evidence that told me these was them times and had always been them times.

Mama had shown us so many of her artifacts, in fact, that by the time people were talking about how hard Black folks (and don't forget the good white folks) fought to open this museum, and how we all needed to go to better ourselves and know our histories, I felt I had seen and heard and inherited enough. In summer 1991 when the Museum opened, I sure smelled like it. I wondered why there had to be a fight to get a museum. I wondered if white folks didn't want there to be a museum because they didn't want us to find out that somebody from right in our town, and not the lone wolf outside agitator James Earl Ray, killed King. That maybe they had done it.

Being 16 when King was killed, Mama spent her whole life knowing. I don't know how many years of extra mourning she was born with. Nor do I know which cataclysmic rupture in the Memphis history that happened to her before she was born—the lynchings of Calvin McDowell, Thomas

Moss, and William Stewart? The burning of Ida B. Wells's newspaper offices?—was the source of that extra mourning. Growing up, Mama's stories of her every day and emotional life after that Thursday, April 4, 1968, made me know that she was herself a museum, archiving all the things of her life and rotating what was on view. She was the docent of her life and of Black southern women's lives and Black Memphis life, guiding us through her exhibits. Mama was an activist for being a museum and for just thinking she deserved freedom. She taught us the Black folk cogito: I think therefore I am free.

Every time we came out of that place, musty and ashy with grief from what the museum said the white folks did to our mamas and grandmas and other folks who looked like us, we were sad and heavy as a patch of winter interrupting a good spring. Even though we had learned that we were a people of hope and resilience and we kept on fighting and pushing and moving and singing spirituals, precious Lord, we still had little explanation as to why white folks acted like that towards us for so long, so we tended to think one of us or some of us had done something wrong to earn that treatment. Like when the teacher punish the whole class for talking and say we can't go outside when it was really only Marcellus and Keon talking but won't nobody tell because we'd rather miss recess once than be a snitch forever.

When we got back into the light, we were right back at the scene of the crime, the centerpiece out of which the museum grew northward and westward, an extra arm and an extra leg. We came fresh out into the air funky not with the stank of what happened before to people who looked like us, but rather with the feeling that it was happening to us, too, seeing as we had fewer and fewer white kids in our classes, and some of the remaining ones usually got sick on museum day.

What really did us in afterward was seeing that balcony and getting close enough to it so it could talk shit to us. People used to say the stain of King's blood was still there from 1968 and that you could see it and the spatter in the concrete outside of the room if you squinted and stretched your neck. That balcony said, you don't know nobody being murdered by white folks like this now, knocked clean up out they shoes. Nobody blood on the concrete now. Act right and read To Kill a Mockingbird. Except you, skinny little you, want to tell that balcony about your cousin who got shot because the police say he pulled a gun on them, but the autopsy say the bullets entered his back. That balcony said to us, this is what will happen to y'all ashy ass if you speak out, too. And also, you free now, so be grateful and take your math test seriously and register to vote. It also said, by this blood, white people have been made maybe a little bit less likely to explicitly infringe on your First Amendment rights. James Earl Ray was just one sick white man, not at all representative of all white folks. Your cousin was a bad Black boy called Boo who thought he was free. James Earl Ray and those cops that pull us over and threaten us and the cops that beat Rodney King (maybe folks are just really mad at people whose last names are King?) are anomalies, bad apples, who just haven't yet been to the museum. Even though they were living in houses and spending money that was the rotten spoil of what they had done to Black people, most white folks just didn't know what some of them had done to us. The textbooks kept them ignorant of the role they had played and how they benefited, so it really wasn't their fault that they didn't know. But now they know so everything is repaired now. White people are better now because of this museum. By His blood on the balcony—can you see it there? Look harder—all lives are saved.

We wasn't actually allowed to tell nobody we was tired afterwards, in our bones and blood, so we kept our weariness deep inside us, simmering on low with a little salt. We were the young, strong inheritors of King's dream, made flesh through our grit and grind and good grades. We had a lot of opportunities our daddies and grandmama 'nem didn't have. Like the opportunity to not be terrorized with dogs or hoses or white ladies with their mouths pulled wide open with wishes for our deaths, only with bullying and displacement and resentment, when we try to go to school with them. Or the opportunity to live in neighborhoods the white folks left in good condition for us, even though they might have been adjacent to chemical plants. And, of course, and perhaps most important, we now have the opportunity to wonder, wander, wonder, through the simulacra of post-racial America, whether that unjust thing that happened to us (when white folks were coincidentally involved) had to do with our race or our individual karma.

We also wasn't really allowed to be mad about the death of King or what we had seen in that museum, just like we wasn't allowed to say we was tired. It was time for our sack lunch on the sidewalk under that wreath, under that balcony. You have more opportunities now. Wasn't no museums like this when we were growing up. (But my Mama is a museum, and I know my grandmama was a museum when she was only a mama.) You better stop mumbling under your breath. Anyway, like Jesus you know from Sunday School and from listening outside your auntie door at night when her friend is over, Martin Luther King, Jr., was a King who did miracles. And like Jesus, he was destined to die. That was just that. He died for our sins of protesting and rioting that brought him here and embarrassed him when he was here. His prophecy came in dreams. He went to the mountaintop in them. And he died so we could be free. Say your grace over your sack lunch. Be glad you got a sack lunch.

Ms. Jacqueline Smith was down there across from the Museum talking about gentrification before white folks even came up with terms like "preservation" and "revitalization" to describe the foolproof Negro removal in which they had been engaged since the 1950s in downtown Memphis. We didn't know what gentrification was because we lived in neighborhoods white folks would never be interested in, in the neighborhoods they had fled on their ever-extending trek to the east of the city. But Ms. Jackie did, and she knew the Museum was part of it way before the first brewery popped up. She knew the end of the Lorraine meant the inevitable end of all kinds of low-income housing, and therefore Black housing, around downtown. Atlanta had begun the demolition of housing projects to make room for Olympic possibilities. Memphis would be next, and there would be no affordable housing for us. King would have wanted affordable housing instead of a Museum, she would say.

They never let us get close to Ms. Jackie on the school fieldtrips, but we might sneak as close as we dared if we finished our sack lunches early and the teachers were still huddled talking while we waited for the yellow buses to come and take us back to our segregated schools. She had worked as a clerk at the Lorraine Motel and also lived there for a time, we learned in our brief conversations with her, always looking over the shoulder to see if the teachers were looking. When the Lorraine closed in the 1970s, she did not imagine it would return as what she might call a worship site for King's death. The Museum was like a long Groundhog Day funeral, King living and then dying and then being resurrected by each visitor to die again on the balcony. Ms. Jackie, her signs, her table, her literature, her seats, her sofa—they were all artifacts of a protest present and future. Her signs told us this museum was wrong and we were wrong for looking for King's bloodstains. We needed more than our Mama Museums, who would get fragile. But we needed places to live, too. I didn't know then that Jackie was the real museum to visit.

By 18, we had stopped going to the museum like we stopped going to church (or at least our Mama or grandma 'nem church) after we moved out from under grown folks' roof. The museum hadn't changed much, but we had in the nine years since it had opened, over those nine years of semi-annual trips: inside to learn about a lot of white bad apples and the resilience and hope of our heroes and leaders, outside ashy to squint at bloodstains, down to pray over our sack lunches under the balcony, and over to ease our musty selves close to Jackie, curious to learn something we hadn't in the museum. The clash of its sameness and our difference made us impatient with its fixity. In particular, I had learned how truly gangsta Rosa Parks was, and I was fire hot with how they had her stone figure sitting there. I knew damn well she ain't want to be no stone figure, and I knew damn well how much restraint it took for her not to beat that bus driver every night.

When the Museum opened the conspiracy appendage of itself across the street in the building where James Earl Ray allegedly took that shot, or where he said he took it and then later said he didn't, it was clear the Museum had doubled down on the themed experience of this One Spectacular Black Death. From that building, you could look out onto the balcony just like James Earl Ray said he did then didn't, aim your eyes at the wreath outside Room 306 like a posthumous target, and imagine what Ray, a bad apple, was thinking before he might have done it.

Then when the Museum redesigned itself in the Obama era, bringing in the best Negro historians from all over the country to gentrify the story of civil rights, it was clear it had doubled down on the interests of its white funders and the containment of history in a dark building, rather than pivoting towards the diverse Black history happening right then, bright and messy in the now Memphis streets. Stationed in the "Black Power" section of the Museum last fall to provide some additional context for students matriculating the liberal arts college that semester, I watched on loop a video that subsumed the Black Lives Matter movement, perhaps the clearest contemporary tie to the Museum's narrative, under an umbrella of "global protest" that included all kinds of uprisings of the decade. There is only one movement, however diversely populated, concerned explicitly with eradicating anti-Blackness from the core of our nation's social institutions, I told the freshmen, these new Memphians I had influence over and desperately needed to be on the side of now Memphis.

When those good Negro historians came, unaware of the now Memphis, the Museum underwent its own kind of internal gentrification, or revitalization, in tandem with the changes around it. Long a bastion of the respectable history of the civil rights movement, and in particular a proponent of respectable, non-violent forms of protest, it increasingly applied these logics to its interpretation of Black Memphians and its interpretation of itself as a social justice brand. It brought James Pate's charcoal series "Kin Killing Kin," which depicts young Black men in Ku Klux Klan hats in the act of shooting each other, to provoke a conversation about youth violence, or, to divert attention from its complicity in conditions that destabilize Black communities. Most recently, at the behest of funders, it attempted to silence a journalist's structural critiques of ongoing racial disparities in Memphis. We belong in the Museum less now than we did on our school fieldtrips.

Maybe that's what Ms. Jackie was trying to tell us about gentrification. I would call the condos that have gone up around the Museum, around the site of King's last breath, "luxury" because that is the parlance today that lets everyone know that we are now talking gentrification, displacement, and inequality. But there's nothing luxury about the trite, overpriced white boxes with their kitschly refurbished historic exteriors that people are willing to live in to avoid poor people and Black people and especially poor Black people. Jackie had called the Museum a tourist trap, but they called it an anchor institution, a community good, a force for change, a site of social justice. They talked about it in terms of tourist dollars and economic impact. An arts district grew up around it, complete with warehouses-turned-artist-housing, galleries, microbreweries, fine dining, yoga studios, and distilleries. The Museum is the Black hole around which this constellation of white economies, the ones of new Memphis, thrives.

Memphis might be the only chocolate city in which the quintessential Martin Luther King, Jr. Boulevard is not in a Black neighborhood. That's because its new name came after Black folks had mostly been moved away already, after Obama was president. Its renaming encourages and emboldens the gentrification along its two miles, which begins in the east near the medical district, passes the FedEx Forum basketball arena, and ends at the river. I be sitting at the bar at the southeast intersection of Main and Martin Luther King, Jr. Avenue and having a $12 cocktail with my last cash and looking out the window and seeing that sign and thinking, "Thank you, Dr.

Martin Luther King," for the money to enjoy this rosemary garnish in this bar with mostly white patrons and white owners and white staff. If I am lucky, I'll get a new Memphis job at a company that will rent out the Museum for a fun end-of-the-year event so we can have an opportunity to go there without an ancestral or curricular imperative. Though one of my white co-workers might regale me with their love and knowledge of civil rights history and how their "kinda conservative" parents were brought to tears when they brought them to the Museum and so forth, those microaggressions will be a small price to pay for a less dutiful sort of trip to the Museum. Or maybe I won't never have one of those new Memphis jobs. Syke. New Memphians don't have cousins who been shot by the police or daddies whose noses were broken by the county cops. Maybe new Memphians don't have cousins at all.

What is the mood like in Memphis 50 years after the assassination of King? What's it like to be the poorest large Black city in the country and the city that killed a man leading a campaign advocating for poor people at the same time? What about that bankruptcy and environmental racism and foreclosure and infant mortality? How you—is it y'all?—feel about all of this police surveillance? Where is the best barbecue/soul food? You say your little cousin was shot in the back by police before social media? Is the dream continuing here, where his blood was spilled? Is this ground zero for the civil rights movement? Is the dream now a nightmare? How can we keep King's dreams alive? Do you know a sanitation worker? About this mountaintop: Are we there yet? Will we ever get there? Was his blood the magic?

Our mood is that low, salty, stank ass simmer of weariness of the same, that stale mid-summer mustiness, that heaviness of a viscous mourning we haven't been able to put down because King and our cousins and friends are murdered and resurrected to be murdered again. We are tired of unfulfilled dreams, dreams deferred, cranes in the sky, and raisins in the sun. If we must be committed to the grotesque—the spectacle of our deaths as well as of the impunity with which our murderers smile and strut about like roosters—then we want some different kinds of museums. A museum for Duanna Johnson in North Memphis that houses Black trans folks. Ones for Steven Askew in that apartment parking lot not too far for my old high school, for Darrius Stewart on Winchester, for the baby Dorian Harris in that North Memphis yard, and for my cousin Boo in South Memphis, that house young Black folks. Some Mama museums.

We been trying to adjudicate the meaning of the civil rights movement since before we were born, since people died for us to vote, and to sit with white folks, to live with white folks, to have our civil rights, our equal opportunity, our integrated schools, our affirmative action. Or, we have been doing it since the state and its extrajudicial arms, radicalized by the Constitution, have been murdering Black people. We been doing it since 1968. We been wanting to know who really did what and thought what, and to what end, because we are trying to figure out why it didn't take. In Memphis in particular, because we been taught that King's death made us free, we especially have been trying to understand by so many means what exactly went wrong. Moreover, we want to know, what kind of freedom is this? As we lay dying, we here have been unlearning that lie.

CONTRIBUTOR BIOGRAPHIES

Stephen V. Ash is a professor emeritus of history at the University of Tennessee. He has authored or edited twelve books, most of them dealing with the experiences of Southerners White and Black during the Civil War and Reconstruction eras. His most recent is *Rebel Richmond: Life and Death in the Confederate Capital*.

Jennifer Biggs is a veteran journalist and a native Memphian who covered various beats before taking on food in 2003. She worked for *The Commercial Appeal* from 2000-2018, most of that time as the paper's food writer and dining reviewer. She was among the first to join *The Daily Memphian* in mid-2018, where she is the food and dining editor and continues to write about food and dining in Memphis.

Beverly G. Bond is an associate professor of history at the University of Memphis. She is the co-editor of the two-volume, *Tennessee Women: Their Lives and Times* and (with Janann Sherman) of *Memphis in Black and White*, *Beale Street*, and two books on the history of the University of Memphis. She directed, with Susan O'Donovan, the "Memphis Massacre Project" and the two are currently editing *Remembering the Memphis Massacre: An American Story*, a collection of essays presented at the symposium commemorating the 150th anniversary of this event.

Molly Caldwell Crosby is the best-selling author of three books, including *The American Plague: The Untold Story of Yellow Fever*, chosen as a *New York Times* Editor's Pick and Barnes & Noble Discover Great New Writer's award. Crosby graduated from Rhodes College, holds a Master of Arts from Johns Hopkins University, and spent several years working for *National Geographic* magazine.

Geoff Calkins is the sports columnist at *The Daily Memphian* and the host of The Geoff Calkins Show on 92.9FM. He has been chronicling sports in Memphis for more than two decades, has been named best sports columnist in the country five times by the Associated Press Sports Editors, and is a member of the Scripps-Howard Hall of Fame. His chapter is adapted from his book of columns, *After the Jump*.

G. Wayne Dowdy is the senior manager of the Memphis Public Libraries history department. He holds a master's degree in history from the University of Arkansas and is a certified archives manager. He is the author of six books, including *A Brief History of Memphis*, *Crusades for Freedom: Memphis and the Political Transformation of the American South*, *Hidden History of Memphis* and *On This Day in Memphis History*, which was awarded a Certificate of Merit by the Tennessee Historical Commission.

Shelby Foote (1916-2005) was an American historian and author, who wrote *Shiloh: A Novel* among other works based in the South. His epic work, *The Civil War: A Narrative*, a three-volume history of the American Civil War, took him two decades to complete. With roots in the Mississippi Delta, Foote chronicled the radical shift from the agrarian planter system of the Old South to the Civil Rights era of the New South. He became familiar to television viewers as a consultant on the Ken Burns's PBS documentary *The Civil War* in 1990.

Karen B. Golightly is an associate professor of English and director of creative writing at Christian Brothers University in Memphis. She holds an MFA in fiction and a PhD in nineteenth-century British and Irish literature. She is the director of Fresh Reads, Memphis Reads, and Paint Memphis as well as the author of one novel, *There Are Things I Know*.

Aram Goudsouzian is professor of history at the University of Memphis. He writes about race, culture, and politics in American history. His books include *The Men and the Moment: The 1968 Election and the Birth of Partisan Politics in America* and an essay collection co-edited with Charles McKinney, *An Unseen Light: Black Struggles for Freedom in Memphis, Tennessee*.

Timothy S. Huebner, the Sternberg Professor of History at Rhodes College, is the author of *Liberty and Union: The Civil War Era and American Constitutionalism*. In 2018, Prof. Huebner and his students gained national attention when they led a collaborative effort with Calvary Episcopal Church and the National Park Service to erect a marker at the site of the antebellum slave mart operated by Nathan Bedford Forrest.

Charles L. Hughes is the director of the Lynne & Henry Turley Memphis Center at Rhodes College. A historian of race, music and the South, his acclaimed first book *Country Soul: Making Music and Making Race in the American South* was released in 2015. He has published and spoken widely, and teaches courses on the region's cultural and political history.

Earnestine Jenkins is professor of art history at the University of Memphis. Jenkins is a visual culture historian researching the expressive cultures-histories of peoples of African descent using comparative and interdisciplinary methods of analysis. Research interests encompass African American historic photography, the relationship between the arts, politics, and leadership, nineteenth through twentieth century Ethiopia, and visual culture studies in the urban south.

Jonathan Judaken is the Spence L. Wilson Chair in the Humanities at Rhodes College. He is a historian of ideas whose work focuses on race and racism and Jews and Judaism. The author, editor, or co-editor of five books and more than fifty articles, he hosted "Counterpoint," a monthly interview show on WKNO-FM, NPR for the Mid-South, where he now does a weekly segment, "Spotlight on Lifelong Learning."

Daniel Kiel is a professor at the University of Memphis Cecil C. Humphreys School of Law and the director of the documentary film, *The Memphis 13*. He is a native Memphian and a graduate of Memphis City Schools, the University of Texas at Austin, and Harvard Law School. His research addresses issues of educational law and inequality, particularly in Memphis.

Janann Sherman earned her Ph.D. in American history and politics at Rutgers University in New Jersey. She was a professor of history at the University of Memphis for nineteen years, the last nine of which she served as Chair of the History Department. She is the author/co-author of eight books, including *Memphis in Black and White*.

Preston Lauterbach is author of *The Chitlin' Circuit and the Road to Rock N' Roll*, *Beale Street Dynasty: Sex, Song, and the Struggle for the Soul of Memphis*, and *Bluff City: The Secret Life of Photographer Ernest Withers*, and a former Virginia Humanities fellow.

Zandria F. Robinson, PhD is a writer and sociologist whose work focuses on race, popular culture, and the U.S. South. She is the author of *This Ain't Chicago: Race, Class, and Regional Identity in the Post-Soul South* and co-author with Marcus Anthony Hunter of *Chocolate Cities: The Black Map of American Life*. Her work appears in *Rolling Stone*, *Hyperallergic*, *Oxford American*, *Scalawag*, *New York Times* and *The Believer*.

David Waters is a nationally award-winning religion journalist who has worked for *The Commercial Appeal* and *The Washington Post*. He is currently distinguished journalist in residence and assistant director of the Institute for Public Service Reporting at the University of Memphis.

ENDNOTES

1. Introduction: A Counter-Monument to Memphis

1. Sanford Levinson, quoting Catherine McKinnon in *Written in Stone: Public Monuments in Changing Societies* (Durham: Duke University Press, 2018 [1998]), 56.

2. David Lusk Gallery.

4. The Civil War and its Legacy in Memphis

1. Memphis' experience was in many ways unique. Unlike Vicksburg and Petersburg, it never experienced an extended siege that prompted suffering and starvation among its population. Unlike Atlanta, Charleston, and Richmond, it never had to rebuild and recover from devastating fires or loss of population.

2. Christopher Morris, *The Big Muddy: An Environmental History of the Mississippi and Its Peoples from Hernando De Soto to Hurricane Katina* (New York: Oxford University Press, 2012), 9-10; G. Wayne Dowdy, *A Brief History of Memphis*, (Charleston: History Press, 2011), 13-24; Beverly G. Bond and Janann Sherman, *Memphis in Black and White* (Charleston: Arcadia Publishing, 2003), 9-48; Gerald Capers, *The Biography of a River Town — Memphis: Its Heroic Age* (Memphis: Burke's Book Store, 1966), 44-105.

3. Capers, *Biography of a River Town*, 95-105; Sven Beckert, *Empire of Cotton: A Global History* (New York, Knopf, 2015), 98-135; Steven Deyle, *Carry Me Back: The Domestic Slave Trade in American Life* (New York: Oxford University Press, 2005), 42-44. The state of Mississippi, for example, imported an estimated 56,560 enslaved people during the 1850s. See Frederic Bancroft, *Slave-Trading in the Old South* (Baltimore: J.H. Furst Co, 1931), 387.

4. *Williams' Memphis Directory* (Memphis: Cleaves and Vaden, 1860); Jack Hurst, *Nathan Bedford Forrest: A Biography* (New York: Knopf, 1993), 31-67; Bancroft, *Slave-Trading in the Old South*, 250-268; Marius Carriere Jr., "Blacks in Pre-Civil War Memphis," in Carroll Van West, ed., *Trial and Triumph: Essays in Tennessee's African American History* (Knoxville: University of Tennessee Press, 2002), 25.

5. Paul H. Bergeron, Stephen V. Ash, Jeanette Keith, *Tennesseans and Their History* (Knoxville: University of Tennessee Press, 1999), 132-136; "Affair at Memphis, Tenn.," as published in Frank Moore, ed., *The Rebellion Record: A Diary of American Events with Documents, Narratives, Illustrative Incidents, Poetry, Etc.* (New York: D. Van Nostrand, 1868), v. II, 591; Dowdy, *Brief History*, 27-29.

6. Timothy S. Huebner, *Liberty and Union: The Civil War Era and American Constitutionalism* (Lawrence: University Press of Kansas, 2016), 147-154. On Shiloh, see Timothy B. Smith, *Shiloh: Conquer or Perish* (Lawrence: University Press of Kansas, 2016). On the Union campaign on the river, see Gary D. Joiner, *Mr. Lincoln's Brown Water Navy: The Mississippi Squadron* (Lanham: Rowman & Littlefield, 2007).

7. "Detailed Report of Flag-Officer Davis, U.S. Navy, Commanding Western Flotilla," in *Official Records of the Union and Confederate Navies in the War of the Rebellion*, Ser. I, v. 23 (Washington, DC: Government Printing Office 1910), 121.

8. Mayor John Park to C.H. Davis, June 6, 1862, in *Official Records*, Ser. I, v. 23, 121; Warren D. Crandall and Isaac D. Newell, *History of the Ram Fleet and the Mississippi Marine Brigade in the War for the Union on the Mississippi and its Tributaries* (St. Louis: Buschart Brothers 1907), 57-60.

9. U.S. Grant to H.W. Halleck, June 27, 1862, in *Official Records of the War of the Rebellion*, Ser. I, v. 17, Pt. 2, 41; John Bordelon, "Rebels to the Core': Memphians under William T. Sherman," *Rhodes Journal of Regional Studies*, 2 (2005), 8-12.

10. Ellen Davies-Rodgers, *The Great Book of Calvary Protestant Episcopal Church 1832-1972* (Memphis: The Plantation Press, 1973), 244.

11. Bordelon, "Rebels to the Core," 7-36; Joseph H. Parks, "A Confederate Trade Center under Federal Occupation: Memphis, 1862 to 1865," *Journal of Southern History*, 7 (1941), 289-314; John F. Marszalek, *Sherman: A Soldier's Passion for Order* (New York: Free Press, 1993), 188-201; Charles Royster, *The Destructive War: Sherman, Stonewall Jackson, and the Americans* (New York: Knopf, 1991), 106-108; Huebner, *Liberty and Union*, 308. Hopefield, Arkansas—located just across the river from Memphis—suffered a similar fate in February 1863. See David O. Demuth, "The Burning of Hopefield," *Arkansas Historical Quarterly*, 36 (1977), 123-129.

12. Bobby L. Lovett, "The Negro's Civil War in Tennessee, 1861-1865," *Journal of Negro History*, 61 (1976), 38; John Cimprich, *Slavery's End in Tennessee, 1861-1865* (Tuscaloosa: University of Alabama Press, 1985), 49-59.

13. Bond and Sherman, *Memphis in Black and White*, 55; Stephen V. Ash, *A Massacre in Memphis: The Race Riot that Shook the Nation One Year After the Civil War* (New York: Hill and Wang, 2013), 76; Andrew L. Slap, "The Loyal Deserters: African American Soldiers and Community in Civil War Memphis," in Stephen Berry, ed., *Weirding the War: Stories from the Civil War's Ragged Edge* (Athens: University of Georgia Press, 2011), 234-248.

14. John Cimprich, *Fort Pillow, a Civil War Massacre, and Public Memory* (Baton Rouge: Louisiana State University Press, 2005); "Further of the Fort Pillow Massacre, Statements by an Eye Witness," *San Francisco Bulletin*, published as *Daily Evening Bulletin*, May 20, 1864, v. 17, issue 37, 1; Huebner, *Liberty and Union*, 321-322.

15. Bond and Sherman, *Memphis in Black and White*, 53-56; Capers, *Biography of a River Town*, 163-164.

16. Bond and Sherman, *Memphis in Black and White*, 58-60; Ash, *Massacre in Memphis*; Thaddeus Stevens, "Speech on the Fourteenth Amendment," May 10, 1866, in Beverly Wilson Palmer and Holly Byers Ochoa, eds., *Selected Papers of Thaddeus Stevens* (Pittsburgh: University of Pittsburgh Press, 1998), v. 2, 138.

17. Court Carney, "The Contested Image of Nathan Bedford Forrest," *Journal of Southern History*, 67 (2001), 603-612.

18. *The Forrest Monument: Its History and Dedication — A Memorial in Art, Oratory, and Literature* (n.p., 1905), 68.

19. Shelby Foote, *Shiloh: A Novel* (New York: Barnes and Noble Books, 1952), 150. "Forrest's Early Home," The Historical Marker Database, available at https://www.hmdb.org.

20. For the texts of these two new markers, see the Historical Marker Database for "1866 Memphis Massacre," https://www.hmdb.org and "Forrest and the Memphis Slave Trade," https://www.hmdb.org.

6. A City of Corpses: Yellow Fever in Memphis

1. Correspondence to the Honorable William Henry Smith, August 19, 1878, *Diary and Letters of Rutherford Birchard Hayes*, Vol. 3, (1865-1881), ed. Charles Richard Williams (Columbus: The Ohio State Archeological and Historical Society, 1922), 498.

2. Rutherford B. Hayes, *President's Annual Message to Congress*, December 2, 1878.

3. J.M. Keating, *The Yellow Fever Epidemic of 1878 in Memphis, Tenn.* (Memphis: Printed for the Howard Association, 1879), 110.

4. Keating, *The Yellow Fever Epidemic*, 115.

5. "Population of the 100 Largest Urban Places: 1870," U.S. Bureau of the Census website, https://www.census.gov.

6. Charles W. Crawford, *Yesterday's Memphis* (Miami: E.A. Seemann Publishing, 1976), 17-18.

7. Samuel Choppin, "History of the Importation of Yellow Fever into the United States, 1693-1878," *Public Health Papers, American Public Health Association*, Vol. 4 (1877-1878), 197-201.

8. Choppin, "History of the Importation of Yellow Fever," 199.

9. Keating, *The Yellow Fever Epidemic*, 105.

10. Reports of the U.S. Weather Bureau, Memphis (April 1877-October 1879), Mississippi Valley Collection, University of Memphis, Manuscript Coll. 256, Vol. 23-24.

11. Henry Diaz and Gregory J. McCabe, "A Possible Connection between the 1878 Yellow Fever Epidemic in the Southern United States and the 1877-78 El Niño Episode," *Bulletin of the American Meteorological Society*, Vol. 81, Issue 1, 1999.

12. Minutes of the Board of Health, City of Memphis, August 23, 1878, Yellow Fever Collection, Memphis and Shelby County Room.

13. Keating, *The Yellow Fever Epidemic*, 123.

14. Walter Reed and James Carroll, "The Etiology of Yellow Fever," *American Medicine* 3 (1902), 301.

15. "History," Washington Square Park Conservancy, http://washingtonsquareparkconservancy.org.

16. Jim Murphy, *An American Plague: The True and Terrifying Story of the Yellow Fever Epidemic of 1793* (New York: Clarion Books, 2003), 42.

17. Murphy, *An American Plague*, 44.

18. Margaret Humphreys, *Yellow Fever and the South* (Baltimore: The Johns Hopkins University Press, 1992).

19. Keating, *The Yellow Fever Epidemic*, 116.

20. Rev. D.A Quinn, *Heroes and Heroines of Memphis, Or Reminiscences of the Yellow Fever Epidemics* (Providence: E.L. Freeman & Sons, 1887), 190.

21. Keating, *The Yellow Fever Epidemic*, 111.

22. Charles C. Parsons Papers, Box II, and George C. Harris Papers, Series I, 1878, Yellow Fever Collection, Memphis and Shelby County Room.

23. "The Cross and the Sword, A Sermon by Charles C. Parsons," George C. Harris Papers, Series I, 1878, Yellow Fever Collection, Memphis and Shelby County Room.

24. Correspondence dated September 11, 1878, *Sisters of St. Mary at Memphis: With the Acts and Sufferings of the Priests and Others Who Were There with Them during the Yellow Fever Season of 1878* (New York: Printed but not Published, 1879).

25. Correspondence dated August 27, 1878, *The Sisters of St. Mary at Memphis.*

26. Correspondence dated August 27, 1878, *The Sisters of St. Mary at Memphis.*

27. Correspondence dated September 2, 1878, *The Sisters of St. Mary at Memphis.*

28. Keating, *The Yellow Fever Epidemic*, 141.

29. Charles C. Parsons Collection, Box II, Yellow Fever Collection, Memphis and Shelby County Room.

30. William J. Armstrong Family File, Elmwood Cemetery, Memphis.

31. Keating, *The Yellow Fever Epidemic*, 159.

32. Keating, *The Yellow Fever Epidemic*, 116.

33. "The Deadliest, Costliest, and Most Intense United States Tropical Cyclones from 1851 to 2010," and "2017 Update," National Hurricane Center website, https://www.nhc.noaa.gov.

34. "Pearl Harbor History," Pearl Harbor Visitors Bureau website, https://visitpearlharbor.org.

35. 9/11 Memorial and Museum website, https://www.911memorial.org.

36. Crawford, *Yesterday's Memphis*, 47 and 53.

37. "Prevention and Control of Yellow Fever in Africa," World Health Organization report, 1998, 33.

38. *Conclusions of the Board of Experts Authorized by Congress to Investigate the Yellow Fever Epidemic of 1878* (Washington, DC: Judd & Detweiler, Printers, 1879), Library of Congress, Rare Book Collection.

39. *Yellow Fever Bill*, 1879, Library of Congress, Rare Book Collection.

40. "Reported Loss of the Steam-Ship Emily B. Souder," *New York Times*, December 28, 1878.

41. William W. Sorrels, *Memphis' Greatest Debate: A Question of Water* (Memphis: Memphis State University Press, 1970), 45.

42. "Max Theiler Biographical," Nobel Prize Foundation website, https://www.nobelprize.org, and "Yellow Fever," Centers for Disease Control and Prevention website, https://www.cdc.gov.

7. Creativity and Exploitation: A History of the Memphis Economy

1. Robert A. Sigafoos, *Cotton Row to Beale Street: A Business History of Memphis* (Memphis: Memphis State University Press, 1979), 10-11, 32-33; G. Wayne Dowdy, *A Brief History of Memphis* (Charleston: The History Press, 2011), 15-18.

2. Sigafoos, *Cotton Row to Beale Street*, 33-34. Marius Carriere, Jr., "Blacks in Pre-Civil War Memphis," *Tennessee Historical Quarterly*, spring, 1989, 3-14; Frederic Bancroft, *Slave Trading in the Old South* (New York: Ungar, 1959), 250-68.

3. Bancroft, *Slave Trading in the Old South*, 253.

4. Dowdy, *A Brief History of Memphis*, 29-37.

5. Sigafoos, *Cotton Row to Beale Street*, 72, 76-78.

6. Sigafoos, *Cotton Row to Beale Street*, 23-25. Gina Cordell, "Mississippi River Bridges," *Tennessee Encyclopedia*, https://tennesseeencyclopedia.net/entries/mississippi-river-bridges/ accessed January 7, 2019; G. Wayne Dowdy, *On This Day in Memphis History* (Charleston: The History Press, 2014), 40.

7. Sigafoos, *Cotton Row to Beale Street*, 144-45.

8. Dowdy, *On This Day in Memphis History*, 67. Robert Gordon, "The Memphis Jug Band," http://memphismusichalloffame.com/inductee/memphisjugband/ accessed January 7, 2019.

9. Charles L. Hughes, *Country Soul: Making Music and Making Race in the American South* (Chapel Hill: The University of North Carolina Press, 2015), 9-10; Dowdy, *A Brief History of Memphis*, 115-17.

10. Hughes, *Country Soul*, 52-58.

11. Dowdy, *A Brief History of Memphis*, 118.

12. Ibid, 112. Sigafoos, *Cotton Row to Beale Street*, 274.

13. Dowdy, *On This Day in Memphis History*, 124; Sigafoos, *Cotton Row to Beale Street*, 302-03.

14. Dowdy, *A Brief History of Memphis*, 100-01; Sigafoos, *Cotton Row to Beale Street*, 315; International Port of Memphis Website, http://portofmemphis.com/ accessed January 7, 2019.

15. David Flaum, "Limited Recovery Seen for Memphis in MSU Research," *The Commercial Appeal* (Memphis), November 23, 1982.

16. Jessica Silver-Greenberg and Natalie Kitroeff, "Miscarrying at Work: The Physical Toll of Pregnancy Discrimination," *New York Times* (New York), October 21, 2018; Ted Evanoff, "Amazon to Hire 1,500 for Memphis Distribution Centers," *The Commercial Appeal* (Memphis), September 27, 2018.

17. Phillip Jackson, "Indigo Ag to Build North American Headquarters in Downtown Memphis and Bring 700 New Jobs," *The Commercial Appeal* (Memphis), December 12, 2018. Ted Evanoff, "Indigo Will Put Memphis on the Ag Tech Map Like Never Before, *The Commercial Appeal* (Memphis), December 13, 2018; Memphis Chamber of Commerce website - Major Employers, https://memphischamber.com/live-in-memphis/work/major-employers/#1496687509215-681d3829-76ff, accessed January 7, 2019.

8. Memphis Sounds: How Music Shaped Our City and Changed the World

1. Throughout the song, "where it's supposed to be" refers to the Memphis music economy, the city's racial politics, and the general time before the King assassination. "Supposed to Be" performed by Booker T. Jones, North Mississippi All-Stars, Al Kapone, from *Take Me To The River*, directed by Martin Shore (2014; New York: Abramorama).

2. Rushing is here referencing a phrase from H.L. Mencken's descriptions of Memphis. Wanda Rushing, *Memphis and the Paradox of Place: Globalization in the American South* (Chapel Hill: University of North Carolina Press, 2009), 25-26.

3. For histories of Beale Street and its music, see Margaret McKee and Fred Chisenhall, *Beale Black and Blue: Life and Music on America's Main Street* (Baton Rouge: Louisiana State University Press, 1993) and Preston Lauterbach, *Beale Street Dynasty: Sex, Song and the Struggle for the Soul of Memphis* (New York: W.W. Norton, 2015).

4. For example, Handy titled his 1941 autobiography *Father of the Blues*.

5. For a history of Memphis jazz that foregrounds schools and other spaces, see Richard J. Alley, "All That Jazz in the Land of Blues," *Memphis Magazine*, June 3, 2013, found at https://memphismagazine.com/style/all-that-jazz-in-the-land-of-blues/.

6. Thomas made these comments in "40 Years of Memphis Soul," Stax Records press release, January 1971, located in archives of Stax Museum of American Soul Music, Memphis, TN. I later incorporated this and other thoughts from Thomas in my article "'You Pay One Hell of a Price to be Black': Rufus Thomas and the Racial Politics of Memphis Music," in Charles McKinney & Aram Goudsouzian, eds., *An Unseen Light: Black Struggles for Freedom in Memphis, Tennessee* (Lexington: University Press of Kentucky, 2018).

7. For histories of Phillips and Sun, see John Floyd, *Sun Records: An Oral History* (Memphis: Devault-Graves, 2015, 2nd edition) and Peter Guralnick, *Sam Phillips: The Man Who Invented Rock 'n' Roll* (New York: Little, Brown & Co, 2015).

8. The most complete and compelling discussion of Presley's early career is Guralnick's *Last Train to Memphis: The Rise of Elvis Presley* (Boston: Back Bay Books, 1995).

9. The best histories of Stax are Rob Bowman, *Soulsville U.S.A.: The Story of Stax Records* (New York: Schirmer, 2003, second edition) and Robert Gordon, *Respect Yourself: Stax Records and the Soul Explosion* (New York: Bloomsbury, 2013).

10. Robert Gordon offers a rich discussion of these and other artists in his alternative history *It Came from Memphis* (New York: Atria, reprint, 2001).

11. Zandria F. Robinson, "Soul Legacies: Hip-Hop and Historicity in Memphis," from Mickey Hess, *Hip Hop in America: A Regional Guide* (New York: Greenwood, 2009), 549. Robinson expands on these ideas in *This Ain't Chicago: Race, Class and Regional Identity in the Post-Soul South* (Chapel Hill: University of North Carolina Press, 2014).

12. I explore this process and its consequences in my book *Country Soul: Making Music and Making Race in the American South* (Chapel Hill: University of North Carolina Press, 2015).

9. The South's Moveable Feast: Food in Memphis

1. Natasha Geiling, "The Evolution of American Barbecue," https://www.smithsonianmag.com, July 18, 2013.

10. A Brief History of Religion in Memphis

1. "Association of Religion Data Archives, County Membership Report, Shelby County, TN" (2010), Glenmary Research Center, Atlanta.

2. Cecil M. Robeck, *The Azusa St. Mission & Revival: The Birth of the Global Pentecostal Movement* (Nashville: Thomas Nelson, 2006), 220.

3. Ithiel Clemmons, *Bishop C. H. Mason and the Roots of the Church of God in Christ* (Lanham, MD: Pneuma Life Publishing, 1996), 2.

4. Robert Michael Franklin, "My Soul Says Yes, The Urban Ministry of the Church of God in Christ" in Clifford J. Green, ed., *Churches, Cities and Human Community: Urban Ministry in the United States, 1945-1985* (Grand Rapids: William B. Eerdmans Publishing Co., 1996), 77-96.

5. Robert G. Lee. "Payday Someday." newsforchristians.com. (accessed Jan. 30, 2019). http://www.newsforchristians.com/clser1/lee-rg001.html.

6. "Belleue's Lee 'One of the Towering Giants,'" *The Commercial Appeal* (Memphis), July 21, 1978.

7. Patricia M. LaPointe, "The Prophetic Voice: Rabbi James A. Wax" in Mark K. Bauman, Berkley Kalin, eds., *The Quiet Voices: Southern Rabbis and Black Civil Rights, 1880s to 1990s* (Tuscaloosa: University of Alabama Press, 1997), 153.

8. "Rabbis were key players in fight for equal rights," *The Commercial Appeal* (Memphis), March 26, 1995.

11. The Hooks Brothers of Memphis: Artist-Photographers of the "New Negro" Movement in the Urban South

1. For more on the relationship between photography, race, representation and the New Negro Movement, see Deborah Willis, "Representing the New Negro" in Brian Wallis and Deborah Willis, *African American Vernacular Photography* (New York: The International Center of Photography / Gottingen, Germany: Steidel Publisher, 2005), 17–20; Deborah Willis, "Picturing the New Negro Woman," in *Black Womanhood: Images, Icons, and Ideologies of the African Body* (Hanover, New Hampshire: Hood Museum of Art / Seattle and London: Dartmouth College and University of

Washington Press, 2008), 227-245; Paula C. Austin, "'Conscious Self-Realization and Self-Direction': New Negro Ideologies and Visual Representation," *The Journal of African American History*, Volume 103, summer 2018, 309-335.

2. Willis, *African American Vernacular Photography*, 18.

3. Brian Wallis, "The Dream Life of a People: African American Vernacular Photography," in *African American Vernacular Photography*, 9-14.

4. Wallis, "Dream Life of a People," 11.

5. See David Levering Lewis and Deborah Willis, *A Small Nation of People: W. E. B. Dubois & African American Portraits of Progress* (Washington, DC: Library of Congress, 2003); Shawn Michelle Smith, *Photography on the Color Line: W.E.B. Dubois, Race, and Visual Culture* (Durham & London: Duke University Press, 2004); Eugene F. Provenzo Jr., *W.E.B. Dubois's Exhibit of American Negroes: African Americans at the Beginning of the Twentieth Century* (Lanham, Maryland: Rowman & Littlefield, 2013).

6. Library of Congress. Subject category is African American Photograph assembled for 1900 Paris Exposition, and under African American dwellings, LC-USZ62-51561, call # Lot 11307

7. Annette Church and Roberta Church, *The Robert R. Churches...*, 41.

8. Ibid., 33-34.

9. Ibid., 33.

10. George W. Lee, *Beale Street: Where the Blues Began* (New York: Robert O. Ballou, 1934), 197.

11. G.P. Hamilton, *The Bright Side of Memphis* (Memphis: G.P. Hamilton, 1908).

12. Hamilton, *Bright Side of Memphis*, 245.

13. Michael Bieze, *Booker T. Washington and the Art of Self-Representation* (New York: Peter Lang, 2008).

14. Austin, *New Negro Ideologies and Visual Representations*, 316.

15. Pamela Palmer, ed., *The Robert R. Church Family of Memphis: Guide to the Papers with Selected Facsimiles of Documents and Photographs* (Memphis: Memphis State University Press, 1979), 8-13.

16. For more on Church see Annette Church and Roberta Church, *The Robert R. Churches...*

17. Church Family Papers, University of Memphis.

18. Thomas O. Fuller, *Pictorial History of the American Negro* (Memphis: Pictorial History, Inc., 1933).

19. See Alan Trachtenberg's chapter, "Illustrious Americans," in *Reading American Photographs: Images as History Matthew Brady to Walker Evans* (New York: Hill and Wang, 1989), 21-70.

20. Shawn Michelle Smith, *Photography on the Color Line; W. E. B .Dubois, Race, and Visual Culture* (Durham: Duke University Press, 2005), 66-67.

21. For a discussion about the linkage between depicting racial progress and middle-class manhood in photographic portraiture, see Marlon B. Ross, "The Arrested Gaze: The Race Album and the Fraternal Look of the New World Negro," in *Manning the Race: Reforming Black Men in the Jim Crow Era* (New York and London: New York University Press, 2004), 61-77.

22. Miriam DeCosta-Willis, *Black Memphis Landmarks* (Jonesboro, Arkansas: GrantHouse Publishers, 2010), 42.

23. *The News Scimitar*, January 22, 1919.

24. This photograph was one of thirty pictures used to illustrate African American patriotism during World War I in Miles Vandahurst Lynk, *The Negro Pictorial Review of the Great World War; a Visual Narrative of the Negro's Glorious Part in the World's Greatest War* (Memphis: Twentieth Century Art Company, 2019), 36.

25. DeCosta-Willis, *Black Memphis Landmarks*, 97.

26. Miriam DeCosta Willis, *Notable Black Memphians* (Amherst, New York: Cambria Press, 2008), 232-233.

27. *The Nashville Globe*, September 19, 1913.

28. William J. Breen, "Black Women and the Great War: Mobilization and Reform in the South," *The Journal of Southern History*, Vol. 44, No.3 (Aug., 1978), 437.

29. Austin, *New Negro Ideologies and Visual Representations*, 335.

13. Protest, Politics, and Paradox: The Black Freedom Struggle in Memphis

1. Michael K. Honey, *Going Down Jericho Road: The Memphis Strike, Martin Luther King's Last Campaign* (New York: W.W. Norton, 2007).

2. Michael K. Honey, *To the Promised Land: Martin Luther King and Fight for Economic Justice* (New York: W.W. Norton, 2018); Michael K. Honey, *Southern Labor and Black Civil Rights: Organizing Memphis Workers* (Urbana: University of Illinois Press, 1993); Michael K. Honey, *Black Workers Remember: An Oral History of Segregation, Unionism, and the Freedom Struggle* (Berkeley: University of California Press, 1999).

3. On the sanitation strike see also Joan Turner Beifuss, *At the River I Stand*, 2nd ed. (Memphis: St. Luke's Press, 1990).

4. On early Memphis as a paradox, see Gerald Capers, *The Biography of a River Town: Memphis, Its Heroic Age* (Chapel Hill: University of North Carolina Press, 1939), 207. For broader notions of paradox in modern Memphis see Wanda Rushing, *Memphis and the Paradox of Place: Globalization in the American South* (Chapel Hill: University of North Carolina Press, 2009).

5. Kenneth W. Goings and Brian D. Page, "African Americans versus the Memphis Street Railway Company: Or, How to Win the Battle but Lose the War, 1890-1920," *Journal of Urban History* 30, No. 2 (Summer 2004): 131-151.

6. Darius Young, "'The Saving of Black America's Body and White America's Soul': The Lynching of Ell Persons and the Rise of Black Activism in Memphis," in Aram Goudsouzian and Charles W. McKinney Jr., *An Unseen Light: Black Struggles for Freedom in Memphis, Tennessee* (Lexington: University Press of Kentucky, 2018), 39-60.

7. Paula Giddings, *Ida: A Sword Among Lions* (New York: Amistad, 2008).

8. Darius Young, *Robert R. Church Jr. and the African American Freedom Struggle* (Gainesville: University Press of Florida, 2019).

9. Elizabeth Gritter, *River of Hope: Black Politics and the Memphis Freedom Movement, 1865-1954* (Lexington: University Press of Kentucky, 2014), 1-136; G. Wayne Dowdy, *Mayor Crump Don't Like It: Machine Politics in Memphis* (Jackson: University Press of Mississippi, 2008); Jason Jordan, "We'll Have No Race Trouble Here: Racial Politics and Memphis's Reign of Terror," in Goudsouzian and McKinney, *An Unseen Light*, 130-149.

10. Laurie B Green, *Battling the Plantation Mentality: Memphis and the Black Freedom Struggle* (Chapel Hill: University of North Carolina Press, 2007), 47-226; Elizabeth Gritter, "Black Memphians and New Frontiers: The Shelby County Democratic Club, the Kennedy Administration, and the Quest for Black Political Power, 1959-1964," in Goudsouzian and McKinney, *An Unseen Light*, 177-202; G. Wayne Dowdy, *Crusades for Freedom: Memphis and the Political Transformation of the American South* (Jackson: University Press of Mississippi, 2010), 33-107.

11. Sherry L. Hoppe and Bruce W. Speck, *Maxine Smith's Unwilling Pupils: Lessons Learned in Memphis's Civil Rights Classroom* (Knoxville: University of Tennessee Press, 2007), 23-132; Daniel Kiel, "Lessons from *The Memphis 13*: What 13 First-Graders Have to Teach About Law, Life, and the Legacy of Brown," *Thurgood Marshall Law Review* 39, no. 1 (Fall 2013): 63-117.

12. Green, *Battling the Plantation Mentality*, 233-241; Steven A. Knowlton, "'Since I Was a Citizen, I Had the Right to Attend the Library': The Key Role of the Public Library in the Civil Rights Movement in Memphis," in Goudsouzian and McKinney, *An Unseen Light*, 203-227; Elizabeth Gritter, *Memphis Voices: Oral Histories on Race Relations, Civil Rights, and Politics* (New Albany, IN: Elizabeth Gritter Publishing, 2016), 105-150.

13. Green, *Battling the Plantation Mentality*, 251-287; Shirletta J. Kinchen, *Black Power in the Bluff City: African American Youth and Student Activism in Memphis, 1965-1975* (Knoxville: University of Tennessee Press, 2016), 45-116; Anthony C. Siracusa, "Nonviolence, Black Power, and the Surveillance State in Memphis's War on Poverty," in Goudsouzian and McKinney, *An Unseen Light*, 279-305.

14. Kinchen, *Black Power in the Bluff City*, 143-173; James Conway, "Beyond 1968: The 1969 Black Monday Protest in Memphis," in Goudsouzian and McKinney, *An Unseen Light*, 306-329.

15. Marcus D. Pohlmann, *Opportunity Lost: Race and Poverty in the Memphis City Schools* (Knoxville: University of Tennessee Press, 2008), 63-90. See also J. Scott Frizzell, "The Impossible, Only Solution: School Busing and Racial Integration in Memphis, Tennessee, 1972-1975" (Ph.D. diss., University of Memphis, 2016). On the longer history of race and education in Memphis see Beverly Bond, "Educating the 'Common Man': Developing Public School Systems in Memphis and Shelby County, 1820 to 1954" in John M. Amis and Paul M. Wright, *Race, Economics, and the Politics of Educational Change* (Knoxville: University of Tennessee Press, 2018), 21-56.

16. Sharon D. Wright, *Race, Power, and Political Emergence in Memphis* (New York: Garland, 2000), 85-122.

17. Otis Sanford, *From Boss Crump to King Willie: How Race Changed Memphis Politics* (Knoxville: University of Tennessee Press, 2017), 203-242; Marcus D. Pohlmann and Michael P. Kirby, *Racial Politics at the Crossroads: Memphis Elects Dr. W. W. Herenton* (Knoxville: University of Tennessee Press, 1996).

18. Charles W. McKinney Jr., "Coda," in Goudsouzian and McKinney, *An Unseen Light*, 393-399; Michael K. Honey, "Black Workers Matter: The Continuing Search for Racial and Economic Equality in Memphis," in Goudsouzian and McKinney, *An Unseen Light*, 366-392. On Black culture and identity in Memphis, see also Zandria F. Robinson, *This Ain't Chicago: Race, Class, and Regional Identity in the Post-Soul South* (Chapel Hill: University of North Carolina Press, 2014).

14. Beauty and Bitterness: Two Centuries of Memphis Education

1. Gerald M. Capers, *The Biography of a River Town: Memphis, It's Heroic Age* (New Orleans: Tulane University Press, 1966), 72.

2. Beverly Bond. "Educating the 'Common Man': Developing Public School Systems in Memphis and Shelby County, 1820 to 1954," in *Race, Economics, and the Politics of Educational Change: The Dynamics of School District Consolidation in Shelby County, Tennessee*, ed. John M. Amis and Paul M. Wright (Knoxville: University of Tennessee Press, 2018), 24.

3. Marcus D. Pohlmann, *Opportunity Lost: Race and Poverty in the Memphis City Schools* (Knoxville: University of Tennessee Press, 2008), 42.

4. Bond, "Educating the 'Common Man': Developing Public School Systems in Memphis and Shelby County, 1820 to 1954," 26.

5. Bond, "Educating the 'Common Man': Developing Public School Systems in Memphis and Shelby County, 1820 to 1954," 26-27.

6. Bond, "Educating the 'Common Man': Developing Public School Systems in Memphis and Shelby County, 1820 to 1954," 29.

7. W.W. Herenton, "A Historical Study of School Desegregation in the Memphis City Schools, 1954-1970," (Ph.D. diss., Southern Illinois University, 1971), 53; Daniel Kiel, "Exploded Dream: Desegregation in the Memphis City Schools," *Law and Inequality: A Journal of Theory and Practice* 26 (2) (2008): 270.

8. Kiel, "Exploded Dream," 265.

9. Daniel Kiel, "Lessons from *The Memphis 13*: What 13 First-Graders Have to Teach About Law, Life, and the Legacy of Brown." *Thurgood Marshall Law Review* 39 (1) (2013): 73.

10. Kiel, "Lessons from *The Memphis 13*," 73.

11. Kiel, "Lessons from *The Memphis 13*," 77.

12. Daniel Kiel, *The Memphis 13*, https://thememphis13.com, 2011.

13. Kiel, *The Memphis 13*.

14. Kiel, "Lessons from *The Memphis 13*," 78-79.

15. Kiel, "Exploded Dream," 285.

16. Mark Newman, *Desegregating Dixie: The Catholic Church in the South and Desegregation, 1945-1992*, (Oxford: University Press of Mississippi, 2018), 182-83; Jane Roberts, "How Brother Terence McLaughlin Helped Transform Memphis," *Memphis Magazine*, September 17, 2018.

17. Kiel, "Exploded Dream," 286-87.

18. Daniel Kiel, "A Memphis Dilemma: A Half-Century of Public Education Reform in Memphis and Shelby County from Desegregation to Consolidation," *University of Memphis Law Review* 41 (4) (2011): 798.

19. Robert M.McRae, "Oral History of the Desegregation of Memphis City Schools 1954-1974," (1997), 91.

20. Pohlmann, "Opportunity Lost," 83.

21. Kiel, *The Memphis 13*.

22. Kiel, "A Memphis Dilemma," 815.

23. Elena Delavega, "The Poverty Report: Memphis Since MLK: How African Americans and the Poor Have Fared in Memphis and Shelby County Over the Past 50 Years" (Memphis: National Civil Rights Museum, 2018), 8.

24. Delavega, "The Poverty Report," 13.

25. Vernon Brundage, Jr., "Profile of the Labor Force by Educational Attainment," (Washington: United States Bureau of Labor Statistics. https://www.bls.gov/spotlight/2017/educational-attainment-of-the-labor-force/pdf/educational-attainment-of-the-labor-force.pdf , 2017), 8.

26. Kiel, *The Memphis 13*.

15. The Tigers, the Grizzlies, and the City We Wish to Be

1. Wendi Thomas, "Stop using basketball as a Band-aid for racial progress," *The Undefeated*, May 11, 2017, https://theundefeated.com/features/stop-using-basketball-as-a-band-aid-for-racial-progress/.

2. Zach Mcmillin, "Memphis State: quite a commitment," *The Commercial Appeal*, March 30, 2003, http://www.zackmcmillin.com/wp-content/uploads/2012/09/TimelessTigers.FullSeries.pdf.

3. Zach Mcmillin, "1973 - All the Way - Tigers didn't waltz into UCLA meeting, " *Memphis Tigers Men's Basketball*, April 6, 2008. http://uofmtigers.blogspot.com/2008/04/1973-all-way-tigers-didnt-waltz-into.html.

4. Ibid.

5. Zach Mcmillin, "Memphis State: quite a commitment," *The Commercial Appeal*, March 30, 2003, http://www.zackmcmillin.com/wp-content/uploads/2012/09/TimelessTigers.FullSeries.pdf

6. Chris Herrington, "Herrington: Mike Conley is the last man standing, and an era of Grizzlies basketball is over," *The Daily Memphian*, February 11, 2019, https://dailymemphian.com/article/3005/Herrington-Mike-Conley-is-the-last-man-standing-and-an-era-of-Grizzlies-basketball-is-over.

7. Tom Charlier, "Iwo Jima battle survivor from Memphis making return trip," *The Commercial Appeal*, February 18, 2015, http://archive.commercialappeal.com/news/iwo-jima-battle-survivor-from-memphis-making-return-trip-ep-941284497-324459231.html/.

8. Geoff Calkins, "No title run, but Grizzlies' season had a beat you could dance to," *The Commercial Appeal*, May 15, 2015, http://archive.commercialappeal.com/columnists/geoff-calkins/geoff-calkins-no-title-run-but-grizzlies-season-had-a-beat-you-could-dance-to-ep-1085533693-324397841.html.

NOTES